MAIN STREET

The Face of Urban America

MAIN STREET

The Face of Urban America

by Carole Rifkind

HARPER & ROW, PUBLISHERS
New York Hagerstown
San Francisco
London

MAIN STREET: THE FACE OF URBAN AMERICA. Copyright © 1977 by Carole
Rifkind and Carole Rifkind as Trustee. All rights reserved. Printed in the
United States of America. No part of this book may be used or reproduced
in any manner whatsoever without written permission except in the case of
brief quotations embodied in critical articles and reviews. For information
address Harper & Row, Publishers, Inc., 10 East 53rd Street, New York,
N.Y. 10022. Published simultaneously in Canada by Fitzhenry & Whiteside
Limited, Toronto.

FIRST EDITION

Designed by C. Linda Dingler

Library of Congress Cataloging in Publication Data
Rifkind, Carole.
  Main street.
  Bibliography: p.
  Includes index.
  1. Cities and towns—United States—History.
2. City and town life—United States—History.
3. Cities and towns—United States—Pictorial
works. I. Title.
HT123.R53   1977   301.36′3′0973   76-5527
ISBN 0-06-013573-5

77 78 79 80   1 2 3 4 5 6 7 8 9 10

Contents

Acknowledgments

Many people have kindly helped in the preparation of this book. I am very grateful to the archivists, curators, librarians, collectors and others who conscientiously and resourcefully assisted in locating photographs and in answering repeated questions and queries. For their special efforts on my behalf, I would like to thank Eve Anderson, Valentine Museum; James E. Anderson, University of Louisville; David Bagley and Jack D. Haley, University of Oklahoma; Barbara Bartos, Geneva (New York) Historical Society; Babette Beach, Junction City (Kansas) Public Library; Leroy Bellamy and Jerry L. Kearns, Division of Prints and Photographs, Library of Congress; Jean Bible, Dandridge, Tennessee; Betty Callaway, Selma, Alabama; Marie Chorazy, Umatilla County (Oregon) Library; John Collins, Marshall (Michigan) Historical Society; Peg Dann, Cincinnati Historical Society; Lori Davisson, Arizona Historical Society; Eugene D. Decker, Kansas State Historical Society; Thomas G. De Claire, Map Division, Library of Congress; Robert E. Doran, Geneva, New York; John Ellingsen, Bovey (Montana) Restorations; Richard H. Engeman and Janice Worden, Oregon Historical Society; David Featherstone, University of Oregon; Ron Flemming, Vision, Inc., Boston; Mike Forrester, Editor, *East Oregonian*, Pendleton; Margot Gayle, New York; Frank L. Green, Washington State Historical Society; Margaret Groner, Kansas Collection, University of Kansas; Gail Guidry, Missouri Historical Society; Mary Michel Hamel,

Kentucky Historical Society; Laura Hayes, Wyoming State Archives; C. E. Helfter, Buffalo and Erie County (New York) Historical Society; Barbara Ide, St. Joseph, Missouri; Melanchthon W. Jacobus, The Connecticut Historical Society; David J. Johnson, Michigan State Archives; Joyce Ketcham, Crawford County (Pennsylvania) Historical Society; William Leary, National Archives; Margaret Lester, Utah State Historical Society; Irene Lichens, The Society of California Pioneers; Jean Penn Loerke, Waukesha, Wisconsin; Daniel Lohnes, Society for the Preservation of New England Antiquities, Boston; Paul J. McGinley, Anderson Notter Associates, Boston; Norman Mintz, Market Street Restoration Agency, Corning, New York; Ron Neely, Historic Georgetown (Colorado), Inc.; Paula Oyama, Raymond, Parish and Pine, Inc., Tarrytown, New York; William B. Pinney, Vermont Division for Historic Preservation; David Plowden, Sea Cliff, New York; Virginia Remington, Andover (Massachusetts) Historical Society; Melodie Rue, State Historical Society of Wisconsin; June Sampson, Herkimer County (New York) Historical Society; Marion Terry, Suffolk County (New York) Historical Society; Alan Weiner, New York, New York; Bonnie Wilson, Minnesota Historical Society; Howard W. Wiseman, The New Jersey Historical Society; Daniel A. Yanchisin, Memphis/Shelby County Public Library; Carol Zabilski, University of Washington.

In addition, Richard Russack, founder of the National Stereoscopic Association (RFD 1, Fremont, New Hampshire)—a collector's organization and information source—has been gracious in opening to me his fine collection of stereographs and in permitting their publication in this book.

For the generous gift of their time in reading all or part of my manuscript and for their valuable advice, suggestions and comments I would like to express my gratitude to G. David Brumberg, Geneva, New York; James Marston Fitch, Columbia University; Deborah Gardener, New York City Landmarks Preservation Commission; Tucker Hill, Virginia Historic Landmarks Commission; John Jeffries, Junction City, Kansas; Louise Johnson, Stillwater, Minnesota; Carol Levine, Hastings-on-Hudson, New York; Mary C. Means, National Trust for Historic Preservation; Waible E. Patton, Pendleton,

Oregon; John Peterson, Harvard University; Adolf Placzek, Columbia University; Barbara Quinn, New York; Tyler Smith, Hartford, Connecticut; George Talbot, State Historical Society of Wisconsin; Marcel Villenueva, Orange, New Jersey; Walter Muir Whitehill, North Andover, Massachusetts.

I am most appreciative for the patience and judgment of my editor, Cass Canfield, Jr. For their skill, imagination, and good humor, I am indebted to designer C. Linda Dingler and production editor Carol E. W. Edwards.

My deepest debts are to my mother, who lovingly helped me launch this book, and to my husband, whose enthusiasm, encouragement and keen criticism were essential to its completion.

Introduction

It was called Towne Street when it was a single wilderness road in New England, High Street in a southern New Jersey town, Broad Street in Pennsylvania or South Carolina, Market Street in Ohio, Grand Street in a brash Wyoming city, Broadway in California. But as Main Street, it was uniquely American, a powerful symbol of shared experience, of common memory, of the challenge and the struggle of building a civilization. Through history the name embraced a variety of urban forms—the thickened spine of a New England township, the central street in a neat grid, the city center at the junction of diagonal boulevards, the downtown mall in the remade city of the later twentieth century. Yet Main Street was always familiar, always recognizable as the heart and soul of village, town or city.

This book tells the story of Main Street—its birth, growth and decline. A vital force in the nation's history, Main Street provided tangible proof of progress over three centuries. It is our own generation that seems powerless to sustain the health of our urban environment. We have seen our towns and cities die—strangled by the megalopolis, slashed by the superhighway, buried under urban sprawl. Only in the very recent past—though perhaps too late—have we come to realize that the health of our urban centers depends on the strength that we draw from our past. And Main Street is the historical root of urban America.

Main Street has had as many permutations as there are

towns in the nation and moments in its history. This book does not attempt a complete record; rather, its goal is to draw attention to Main Street as a historic environment, to focus on its significance in the structure of an urban nation, to indicate its essential role in developing a sense of place and local identity.

Social and political history are regularly read in the search for the roots of our national identity; but we have only to *look* with a sensitive and sympathetic eye at the physical evidence of our civilization to *see* urban history. This book uses period photographs (as nearly as possible contemporary with the historic era they were chosen to illustrate) as documents, to show how and why Main Street came to be, and what is happening to it now. Through the veil of time, perhaps we can see Main Street more clearly: ordinary, but richly intricate; humble, but honest; familiar, but fascinating.

From the 1860s, photography was available as a means to record a rapidly changing environment. Main Street was then a vigorous adolescent. From that time through the First World War era, when Main Street enjoyed a healthy maturity, photographic images were made, bought and collected for pleasure, pride and profit. As it reflected the self-image of town or city, Main Street was a natural subject for the photographer. There exist today, scattered among museums, historical societies, newspaper archives, libraries and attic trunks, a wealth of Main Street views, revealing it in almost every stage and aspect.

Of course, photographs alone cannot tell the complete Main Street story. The camera has technical limitations; the photographer's vision is selective; survival, and retrieval, of historic photographs is often fortuitous. But there is still a vast quantity of information, revealing the diversity, complexity and associational richness of the Main Street environment, that can be discovered in photographs. They can show variety of scale, shapes, colors and textures; the skill and ingenuity of the craftsman in wood or masonry; the relation of town to countryside, of building to building, of front to back, of corner to side street. Photographs reveal dynamic changes in social class, ambience, local custom, patterns of use. Through photographs we can experience almost directly the history of a century in the life of Main Street. And with a strong and integrated image of the historic Main Street, perhaps we will better be able to participate in that "continuing dialogue between the generations" which is the nature of urban architecture—and the essence of a civilized society.

ONE

ORIGINS

1. Wilderness

Through most of the colonial period, the agricultural village, half theocracy and half democracy, was the basic form of settlement in New England. "The scene is a novelty in the history of man," said Yale President Timothy Dwight, in preface to his description of his travels through New York and New England in the 1790s and early 1800s. "The colonization of a wilderness by civilized men, where a regular government, mild manners, arts, learning, science, and Christianity have been intertwined in its progress from the beginning, is a state of things of which the western continent and the records of past ages has furnished neither an example, nor a resemblance." By the time of Dwight's travels, the economic simplicity and the religious unity that were basic to the village structure were already beginning to recede, although the physical form of the settlements often remained a remarkably accurate reflection of the principles and traditions that had guided their establishment.

New England villages seemed to grow naturally from their environment. Whether a village was located on a ridge above a river valley, on a gentle southern slope or on a level plain surrounded by wooded hills, town planners respected landscape, topography, orientation, vistas and the nature of the soil and vegetation. Leisurely growth contributed to the grace, charm and beauty of the village. "Because an old-fashioned town . . . grows so slowly and with such extreme deliberation, is the very reason that it seems to have such a delightful completeness when it has entered fairly upon its

3

maturity," recalled novelist Sarah Orne Jewett of her native New England. "The towns which are built in a hurry can be left in a hurry without a bit of regret."

The township grant to a colonizing group might be as large as sixty square miles, but the settlement was usually limited to only a small part. The first clearing in the forest was the village center, the site of the green, the meeting house and a few dozen dwellings. Here the villagers worshiped, made laws, met in social intercourse, and returned each night after a day's work in the outlying fields. "All the people are neighbors: social beings; converse; feel; sympathize; mingle much; cherish sentiments, and are subjects of at least some degree of refinement," wrote Dwight. Distances were measured from the meeting house; early rules specified that no one might live farther from it than a comfortable walk. The village center was surrounded by strip fields, pastures and the as yet uncleared forest. The village and its countryside functioned as a discrete and organic unit.

Medieval traditions, based on functional relationships forthrightly expressed, governed Puritan town-building in the New World. In the first clearing, bounding the village green, sat the square meeting house—replaced, in the later years, by a nave church, crowned by belfry and tower. Marked off along a single street, on lots that varied in size with the need, status and wealth of their owners, were solid wood-framed dwellings which perpetuated Old World craft traditions. At first, this road dead-ended into the countryside, extending only as far as the fields and pastures. But just as the dwelling of the seventeenth century was unabashedly enlarged and altered in the eighteenth or nineteenth century to suit the changing needs of its inhabitants, so the developing pattern of roads, lanes and streets reflected the increasing size, complexity and diversity of New England's villages and towns. The "fferie road," the "mill road," the "road to the hog-house," "Church Street" and the "road to Exeter" branched off at oblique angles from Main Street, ultimately forming a complex pattern of streets and blocks which related more directly to functional needs than to the demands of a neat geometry.

It was anticipated by the founders that an agricultural

Plymouth, Massachusetts, circa 1865
Main Street and square
''Plymouth Views,'' Wm. S. Robbins & Co.
American History Division, New York Public Library, Astor, Lenox and
Tilden Foundations

The church at the head of Main Street is the lineal descendant of the first
Meeting House built by the Pilgrims in Plymouth's Town Square. They had
previously worshipped within the fort on the hill in the background.

Litchfield, Connecticut, circa 1855
Southwest corner of South Street and green
Benedict; Connecticut Historical Society

Settled in the 1720s on what was then the
northwestern frontier, Litchfield grew not only
as a trading center for the surrounding
agricultural region, but also as a site for iron
and clock manufacture and as the seat of
Litchfield County.
Gable end to the front, hotel, store and
courthouse are sited somewhat informally in
relation to each other, the board sidewalk
and the green.

village could accommodate only a limited number of farmers
and that some families would move on to form new communities in the image of the parent. And they did, first in distant
parts of the same township and then farther afield, moving
from the coastal lowlands to the valleys and hills of western
Connecticut and Massachusetts, to the forests of Maine, Vermont and New Hampshire. They moved to the rich flatlands
of the Mohawk Valley and the fertile fields of Ohio, Illinois,
Iowa and Wisconsin in such numbers that it seriously depleted some of the older villages.

By the third or fourth generation, New Englanders turned
away from the covenants that bound their parents' communities; religious beliefs and practices diverged, strangers lived
among them, commerce encroached on agriculture, villages
expanded to the size of towns and small cities. Main Street
became the visual and functional focus of town, although its
character was gradually transformed. An imposing brick or
stone courthouse, bank or town hall crowded the shop,
church and academy. Nearby dwellings were modified to
serve both commerce and trade. Newly built shops, offices
and hotels filled in the Main Street façade. Behind Main

Pawtucket, Rhode Island, circa 1870
Congregational Church
Windsor's Stereoscopic Views
Richard Russack Collection

As roads grew from the town center, the steepled church marked their diverging paths. First settled in 1671, Pawtucket was, in 1793, the site of the nation's first water-powered cotton mill, and grew in the nineteenth century as an industrial suburb of Providence.

Augusta, Maine, circa 1870
Exchange Street from dome of City Building
Richard Russack Collection

A compact grid formed of narrow, irregular streets and small blocks was a plan typical of towns oriented to the sea. Augusta, incorporated in 1797, developed as an important shipbuilding center on the Kennebec River.

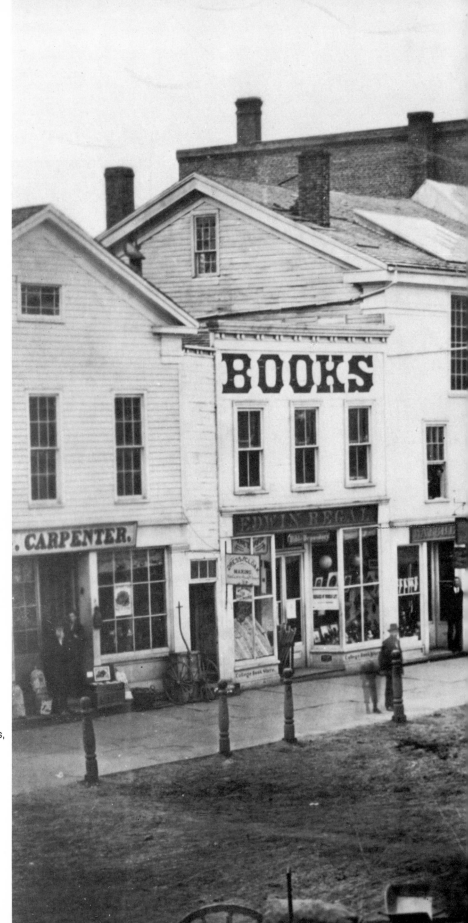

Oberlin, Ohio, circa 1865
Collection of Jane Kosovsky

Settled by New England Congregationalists,
Oberlin prospered as a college town.
(Note the enlarged window opening in the
façade of the photography gallery, cut into
the cornice to achieve more interior light.)

Hartford, Connecticut, circa 1860
Main Street
Delameter; Connecticut Historical Society

In 1636, Hartford began as a compact settlement around an open square. As inhabitants
required new house sites, lots were marked
off the main streets, stretching them farther
and farther from the town center. By the time
of this photograph, though there are gardens
still to be seen behind Main Street houses,
factories are closing in around them. Note
the five-story brick mills in the left
background.

Street, or at its end, clustered mill, forge, stables, tool manufactories and other early industrial enterprises. Sidewalks
were a rare amenity, but pedestrian space was defined and
protected by the great arching branches of the shade trees
that have always been the glory of New England. "I have
not yet been able to ascertain whence arose the ancient practice of thus decorating the streets and high roads," wrote
Theodore Dwight, whose steps retraced the path of his
uncle, "but from my earliest recollections, the fine elms,
spreading their noble branches over my head, excited my
admiration. . . . In many places, particularly in some of the
villages, the finest trees, of extraordinary growth, form two,
three, or four lanes, and overshadow the broad path."

During the first quarter of the nineteenth century, seaport

10

Fitchburg, Massachusetts, circa 1865
Fitchburg Savings Bank block
J. C. Moulton; Richard Russack Collection

Like most New England towns, Fitchburg had long, slow growth as an agricultural community before beginning a period of rapid expansion as a wealthy
industrial city. Side by side, these structures record the change.

Hanover, New Hampshire, circa 1865
Main Street, looking south
"Vermont and New Hampshire Views"
by D. A. Clifford
Society for the Preservation of New England Antiquities

Main Street's trees were dominant elements in New England towns; most memorable were the graceful dark-green canopy of elms (seen here in the foreground) and the brilliant autumn accents of native oak and maple.
Hanover was a farming community in the 1760s, but her fine architecture is the product of the town's prosperity as the home of Dartmouth College.

cities such as Boston, New York, Philadelphia, Baltimore and Charleston experienced remarkable growth, while many inland towns and villages developed as a result of improved land transportation. Main Street stretched many times its original mile or two-mile length, to link one town with the next, to join with the growing network of stage routes, post roads and turnpikes. By the 1820s, there were more than 100,000 miles of roads lacing the East and connecting it to the trans-Appalachian West. The Wilderness Road through the Cumberland Gap opened the way to the lower Ohio Valley; the great Western Road along the Mohawk brought settlers to western New York State and the Great Lakes; the National Road stretched more than six hundred miles to Wheeling on the Ohio River, and beyond to the Illinois prairie. Towns sprang up as if "by the power of enchantment." The through route passed by Main Street; along its

Geneva, New York, circa 1870
Main Street, looking northeast
J. G. Vail; Geneva Historical Society

Geneva was founded in 1797, its Main Street meeting the Genesee Turnpike, the great western route during the stagecoach era.

Providence, Rhode Island, circa 1870
Providence River from Westminster Street
''New England Scenes—American Scenery''
Richard Russack Collection

Founded by Roger Williams, Providence was laid out in 1638 on a linear plan. Long, narrow farm lots extended from the central spine—known first as Towne Street and later as Main Street—down to the Providence River. As new streets were drawn, they followed the boundary lines of the old fields. The town flourished as a trading center in the eighteenth century. By the mid nineteenth century, Westminster Street, at right angles to Main Street, had eclipsed it in commercial activity.

length the colonnaded temple fronts of hotels, churches and public buildings grandly embellished the street façade with the optimism of a young nation.

While many agricultural communities languished in the 1820s and 1830s, some New Englanders found that milling, fishing, trading or shipbuilding were far more rewarding enterprises than farming the thin New England soil. Dozens of new towns sprang up near the rushing rivers that powered their factories. Scores of dwellings were speedily erected in neat rows near the mill site; on Main Street, densely built and specialized commercial structures satisfied the needs of the population that was newly freed from the soil. New Englanders had found that their prosperity was no longer to be found in the land.

The simple street pattern of the New England village was not generally characteristic of settlements elsewhere in the colonies. In the South, a few coastal and river cities flourished, but otherwise settlement there was both sparse and rude. In the Middle States, there developed a greater variety of urban forms, reflecting the cultural crosscurrents and diverse practices of a heterogeneous population. In New York and New Jersey, Main Street did make a fleeting appearance, particularly in villages founded by New Englanders. Prosperous commercial cities grew about old Dutch forts and ports. Good-sized market towns serviced farmsteads spread over a large open-country neighborhood, after the pattern laid down by Dutch and Quaker settlers. An occasional linear village expressed the influence of German settlers, as did the meticulously planned religious communities of the Moravian brethren. As travel increased through the East, informal crossroad settlements developed along the stage routes; a tavern or inn, a smithy and a couple of dwellings provided the nucleus of a small village. But it was principally from New England that Main Street traced its origins, in the century and a half between the first colonial settlement and the nation's independence. As an expression of that time, and that place, Main Street has deep roots in American memory.

Dexter, Maine, circa 1860
Main Street from Zion's Hill
Society for the Preservation of New England Antiquities

In the Maine wilderness, Dexter was founded in 1820 as a company town for
the Amos Abbot Mill operation. Shops command the Main Street; beyond
them are workers' dwellings, and marking the edges of town, the town hall
at the left, and the Baptist Church at the right.

Hope, New Jersey, circa 1880
Intersection of High and Union Streets
Collection of Hester Hartung

The plan for Hope was drawn in 1774 by a bishop of the Moravian Mother
Church in Europe. The village's two main streets meet in an open square on
which face the community's important public buildings. The pillared structure
at the left, built as the communal residence for single females, became the
America House hotel after the failure of the utopian community. The stone
building at the right was first the *Gemeinhaus,* a place of worship and
community social life.

Waldoboro, Maine, circa 1865 (upper left)
Fish Block
Edward A. Wight; Society for the Preservation of
New England Antiquities

By the 1830s, a new building type—the commercial block—is a
familiar Main Street form. Characteristically, the ground story is
given to various commercial users; monolithic granite posts and
lintels permit wide openings for display windows. Upper stories,
for office or dwelling, have identically spaced window openings.

Princeton, New Jersey, 1879 (upper right)
Richard Russack Collection

A Quaker farming settlement in the late eighteenth century,
Princeton flourished as a coach stop on the Philadelphia–New
York route. By the mid nineteenth century, though by-passed by
canal and railroad, the town grew as the home of the college that
bore its name.

Newport, Vermont, circa 1870 (lower left)
Main Street
J. N. Webster; Richard Russack Collection

With their elegant verandahs and mansard roofs, Newport's
stately hotels give no hint of this resort town's earlier history as
a lumbering center.

2. Grid

The settlement of the American continent was a unique episode in the history of urbanization. For nearly 150 years American colonists clung to the shores of the Atlantic, and yet within little more than the half century after nationhood, they planted towns and cities across a wilderness stretching three thousand miles to the Pacific. To accomplish this unprecedented feat, Americans could call on certain attributes characteristic of their civilization: efficiency, opportunism and freedom from the past.

The vast majority of towns laid down in America after the late eighteenth century employed the grid plan, or variations of it. A town plan can hardly be simpler. Basically, the grid consists of rectangular blocks bounded by parallel streets extending in two directions and crossing each other at right angles. Here was a "labor-saving device" without peer: the grid could be planned from a distance, even without exact knowledge of local topography; the grid was easily surveyed and lots conveniently numbered for sale; the grid, rapidly extended in any direction and for any distance, was tailor-made for future growth and exploitation. Not the least of it, the grid plan expressed the order, regularity, balance and predictability most admired by the rationalists of the early nineteenth century.

Penn's impressive grid plan for Philadelphia was widely admired, although in response to the demands of expediency and the provincialism of the American experience, it was generally simplified and abstracted when repeated elsewhere.

Springfield, Illinois, circa 1865
East side of square
Library of Congress

The triangular pediment of the Greek Revival–style Sangamon County Courthouse can be seen behind the trees at the left of this photograph. Typically,
the courthouse is set back from the building line and fronted by a fenced and
shaded lawn.
Springfield's commercial structures are unusually sophisticated, though the
street is as yet unpaved and the sidewalks are wooden. Note the third
building from the right of the photograph, a rare example of a Gothic Revival–
style shopfront.
Springfield was settled in 1818, made county seat a few years later and state
capital in 1837. Abraham Lincoln argued his cases here for a quarter century.
Elected President, he left for Washington in 1861 and never saw Springfield
again.

18

Lexington, Kentucky, 1887
Main Street
Kentucky Historical Society

Lexington's Courthouse Square (on the right) perpetuated an old tradition by also serving as the market square.

For the first "great town" of his colony, Penn provided a grid neatly sited between the Schuylkill and the Delaware rivers. Streets were of a uniform fifty-foot width, except for one-hundred-foot-wide High and Broad streets, which intersected in an open square near the center of the grid. The central square was reserved for the meeting house, the schoolhouse, the statehouse and other public buildings. At the intersection of two major avenues, the public buildings became the focal point of the grid, enhancing its unity and visual identity.

As towns were laid out in the new West, vernacular builders appreciated the practical advantages of the grid, but they also remembered the old villages of New England. The village green became the courthouse square, more often aligned within the pattern of rectangular blocks and avoiding any break in the regularity of the cross streets than ending a street or framing a view. Bounding one side of the square, and perhaps slightly wider than the other streets, was Main Street, now the single axis that dominated the town. A typical midwestern town was described by the journalist Edmund Flagg in 1838: "I was struck by the quiet air of simple elegance which seemed to pervade the place, though its general outlines are those of every other Western village I have visited. One broad, regular street extends through the town, upon either side of which stands the stores and better class

Galena, Illinois, about 1852–1854
Main Street and levee on Galena River
Probably photographed by Alexander Hesler;
Chicago Historical Society

The first steamer entered Galena's river in
1823. The town was laid out a few years
later, its prosperity in the 1830s and 1840s
assured by its activity in the mining and
manufacture of lead and in river trade.
Well-proportioned brick stores and warehouses of that period line Main Street and
the riverfront. They mark a level of sophis-
tication well above contemporary settlements
on the northwestern frontier.

of private residence; while in the background, scattered
promiscuously along the transverse avenues, are log-cabins
surrounded by corn-fields, much like those in the villages of
the French. Three sides of the town are bounded by the
forest, while the fourth opens upon the prairie called the
'String Prairie.' In the center of the village, upon the principal
street, is reserved a square, in the middle of which stands the
courthouse, with other public structures adjacent, and the
stores and hotels along its sides." Efficient and pragmatic,
though lacking in the amenities and leisurely qualities of
eastern settlements, this was the town plan for the new West.

In the trans-Appalachian West there was no history to slow
events, and life was a race for success. An entirely new transportation system, based on the development of fast river
steamboats and an extensive canal network poured a heterogeneous lot of ambitious new immigrants into the area bordering the Ohio and Mississippi rivers and the Great Lakes,

20

Macomb, Illinois, circa 1876
Courthouse Square
Richard Russack Collection

The rapid growth of western towns generated a constant demand for improved public buildings. The first courthouse on this site, built in 1831, was log. The second, begun in 1833, was brick. In 1876, the third McDonough County Courthouse was completed, a grand brick-and-limestone edifice that dominated Macomb's central square and dwarfed the utilitarian brick and frame structures surrounding it.

Cincinnati, Ohio, 1848
Ohio River
Public Library of Cincinnati and Hamilton County

First planned in 1788, Cincinnati boomed as a shipping point for farm products and meat in the 1830s, after the completion of the Ohio and Erie Canal. The homogeneity of building style reflects the rapid growth that took place in those years.

Princeton, Illinois, circa 1870
Immeke's Stereo Views
Richard Russack Collection

Farmsteads in the new West were spread wide on the grid, often at a great distance from each other and from the town center. Princeton was settled in the 1830s by a group from Northampton, Massachusetts.

and brought to eastern markets the produce grown on their fertile farmlands. By 1830, one third of the nation lived west of the Alleghenies. As farming was now a commercial operation, towns developed to serve the needs of the commercial middlemen. Shipping agents, dealers, suppliers, merchants, mechanics, lawyers, doctors and teachers crowded into the brand-new towns. "The rapidity with which a Western village goes forward, and begins to assume importance among the nation, after once having been born and christened, is amazing," reported Flagg. "The mushrooms of a summer's night are but a fit parallel to the growth of the prairie-villages of the Far West." Larger towns grew with dizzying speed; Cincinnati, Louisville, Buffalo, mere villages in the early 1800s, were metropolises by midcentury. "Cincinnati presents an odd spectacle," Tocqueville noted in 1831. "A town which seems to want to get built too quickly to have things done in order. Large buildings, huts, streets blocked by rubble, houses under construction; no names to the streets, no numbers on the houses, no external luxury, but a picture of industry and work that strikes one at every step."

Just as individual towns and cities were packaged by the grid, so was the nation. Efficient exploitation of the vast new continent demanded a convenient method of land organization and distribution. The rectangular survey was the solution. Initiated by order of Congress in 1785, the survey provided that regardless of altitude, land contours, watercourses, rock formation or vegetation, the western territory be divided by parallel lines running east–west and north–south. These would form six-mile-square "townships," which were to be further divided into mile-square "sections" and put up for public sale. With few exceptions, the survey was continued, each year moving farther west, until the six-mile grid was stamped on the face of the continent. Roadways were conveniently located along the boundaries of townships and sections. In the villages that grew up at the right-angled intersections, Main Street was right on the grid.

"Everyone has come to make money," said Tocqueville of the immigrants to the new West. "No one has been born there; no one wants to stay there." Since profit made from speculation in town lots was about the fastest way to accomplish this goal, it is far from surprising that most western towns originated as speculative ventures. An ambitious entrepreneur could buy a parcel of land at a site that seemed to have some natural advantage. Perhaps he could successfully enhance the value of his purchase by promoting it as a county seat or college town. Usually the new town was parceled into lots without regard to social or scenic amenities; civic elements were scaled in proportion to the modest size of commercial lots. The speculator had only to sit back and wait for the profits to roll in. In the 1830s, the mania for speculation in village property was universal. "Common sense was entirely thrown aside in the calculations of village- and city-makers, and impossibilities deemed feasible of execution. On all the rivers, village plots were found staked out at intervals of two or three miles; not only every inland county, but every remote township, had its village, and often scores of them, in

Denver, Colorado, circa 1875
Fifteenth Street from the top of Guard's Hill
Collier's Rocky Mountain Scenery
Richard Russack Collection

Denver was laid out in the 1850s and grew
first as a wooden town. (Note the partial view
of the wooden Gothic cottage at the left.)
After a major fire in 1863 leveled much of
the business district, wood construction was
prohibited. In the rapid growth of the 1870s
and 1880s, Denver rose as a brick city.

Evarts, South Dakota, 1903
Fred W. Smith; W. H. Over Museum

In his autobiographical novel, *A Son of the
Middle Border,* Hamlin Garland tells of his
South Dakota home town on the vast dry-
grass plains, fringed by bare hills: "The village itself was hardly more than a summer
camp, and yet its hearty boastful citizens
talked almost deliriously of 'corner lots' and
'boulevards,' and their chanting was timed
to the sound of hammers."

Hogeland, Montana
Ray-Bell Films, Inc.; American
Geographical Society

The optimism of the land
speculator.

which land was sold by the foot and inch," the journal, *The American Review,* chronicled in 1845. "Each of these places were to be *cities,* and had some remarkable advantages that were possessed by none other, which must bring in a large population. So thought the 'operators.' " The net effect of this profiteering was to plant hundreds of towns and cities which served as magnets for western settlement. The story was repeated endlessly across the continent: in the early 1800s the lure was to western New York and Ohio; in the 1830s to Illinois and Michigan; in the '50s, Kansas; after the Civil War, it was the Dakotas and Nebraska; in the '80s the boom was in southern California; in the '90s the frontier was closed when the Indian lands of the Oklahoma Territory were cut into town lots. In 1818, Morris Birbeck predicted the pattern: "Gain! Gain! Gain! is the beginning, the middle, and the end, the alpha and omega of the founders of American towns. . . ."

Main Street construction was hastened by efficient use of the always scarce labor supply, by utilization of new tech-

Thermopolis, Wyoming, circa 1911
J. E. Stimson; Wyoming State Archives and Historical Department

Thermopolis, founded in the 1870s, was named for its hot springs.

Oklahoma Ave, May 18

Guthrie, Oklahoma Territory,
May 18, 1889
North side of Oklahoma Avenue
A. P. Van Swearingen; Western
History Collection, University of
Oklahoma

nologies and by relentless exploitation of natural resources. The heavy timber house frame of New England, held together by a cumbersome system of mortise, tenon and peg, gave way to the new system of balloon framing developed in the Midwest in the 1830s. Using factory-milled lightweight wooden framing members fastened with machine-made nails, a single carpenter could assemble a building with amazing speed. Wood and iron structural elements could be prefabricated for speedy assembly at the construction site. "There is a firm in Chicago which is happy to furnish cottages and villas, schoolhouses, stores, taverns, churches, courthouses or towns —wholesale or retail—and to forward them, securely packed, to any part of the country," marveled James Parton, correspondent for the *Atlantic Monthly*, in 1867. "No doubt we shall soon have the exhilaration of reading advertisements of these town-makers, to the effect, that orders for the smallest villages will be thankfully received; country towns made to order; a metropolis furnished with punctuality and dispatch."

The will and the way had been found to spread Main Street to every corner of the nation.

On April 22, 1889, the day the Indian lands of the Oklahoma Territory were opened to settlers, a crowd estimated to be as large as fifteen thousand converged on Guthrie in what was undoubtedly the fastest and wildest land grab in American history. A contemporary described the fierce contest to find a site, drive a stake, erect a tent, build a shanty, and thus secure a claim: "One did not know how far to go before stopping; it was hard to tell when it was best to stop, and it was a puzzle whether to turn to the right or the left. Everyone appeared dazed, and all for the most part acted like a flock of stray sheep."

27

3. Trail

MINING

As late as 1840, much of the continent west of the Mississippi was yet unexplored. The geography of this new land was poorly understood, colored by ignorance and rumor. But in the brief span of the next generation, the crisscrossing trails of explorers, surveyors, frontiersmen, drovers, farmers, prospectors and speculators finally filled in the features on the western map.

The discovery of gold in California in 1848 triggered a vast migration across the "Great American Desert." Fifty thousand would-be millionaires made the march over the continent in the following year. Their crusade was an unwritten story as marvelous, according to one enthusiastic contemporary, as any recorded in literature "from the Arabian Nights to the Book of Martyrs." Subsequent mineral discoveries sent prospectors scurrying back across trails through the western mountains, although for most, the strike was always a little farther on or a little higher up. "In every gulch and ravine a tavern was in the process of erection," recalled J. Ross Browne, a correspondent for *Harper's Monthly*, in 1861. "Board and lodging signs over tents not more than ten feet square were as common as blackberries in June; and on

Unidentified California mining town,
circa 1850
Labhard Collection of the University of
New Mexico Art Museum

Restaurant, hotel and boardinghouse are
sited with apparent orderliness along a single
street, although this mining town appears to
be little more than a clearing beside a forest
stream.

San Francisco, California, 1853
Sacramento Street
William Shew; Bancroft Library, University of
California, Berkeley

Four-story brick and masonry buildings,
board sidewalks, kerosene street lights and
at least one multilingual bookstore reveal the
cosmopolitan city that San Francisco had become within a few years of the gold rush.
The settlement's population, 800 in 1848,
soared to nearly 25,000 within two years.

Ophir City, Nevada, circa 1875
William Henry Jackson; Western History
Department, Denver Public Library

Ophir City, a mining town optimistically
named for the biblical city where Solomon's
ships were loaded with gold, was little more
than a temporary trail of log cabins along a
mountain pass.

Dakota Territory, circa 1875
F. Jay Haynes; Richard Russack Collection

Signs are of critical importance in the
rapidly changing streetscape of the mining
boom town—where the morning's muddy
lumber pile is transformed to a two-story
frame before evening.

Though Hartville was an early-twentieth-century iron-mining town, its architectural idiom was hardly different than that of a gold-mining camp two or three generations earlier. Observe the economy of labor achieved by the false front, a method of construction that eliminates the time-consuming measuring and cutting that would be required to fill in a gable end.

no part of the road was there the least chance of suffering from the want of whiskey, dry-goods or cigars." In 1859, the rush for gold led to Pikes Peak, and the next year, the fabulously rich Comstock silver lode was uncovered on the western slopes of the Sierra Nevada. In *Roughing It,* Mark Twain described a Nevada town: "It was a 'wooden' town; its population two thousand souls. The main street consisted of four or five blocks of little white frame stores which were too high to sit down on, but not too high for other purposes; in fact, hardly high enough. They were packed close together, side by side, as if room were scarce in that mighty plain. The sidewalk was of boards that were more or less loose and inclined

Omaha, Nebraska, circa 1870
Frank E. Currier; Richard Russack Collection

Omaha, founded in 1854, grew as a supply station for the westward migration, and after 1869, as a railroad and industrial center as well. Wooden false fronts of the early period yielded rapidly to monumental brick buildings. Note the brick building under construction at the far end of the street.

32

to rattle when walked upon. In the middle of the town, opposite to the stores, was the 'plaza' which is native to all towns beyond the Rocky Mountains—a large unfenced, level vacancy, with a liberty pole in it. . . ."

The human stampede moved on the Snake River Valley in Idaho and Last Chance Gulch in Montana, and finally over the ancestral lands of the Sioux in the Black Hills of Dakota. Copper was discovered in Wyoming in the 1880s and in the Klondike in the 1890s. But this was about the last of the great mining rushes. Thereafter, mining became big business, operated by well-capitalized organizations which could afford the large-scale machinery needed to make mining profitable.

Mining towns were transitory; few prospectors and camp followers had any intention of making them a permanent home. Thousands of mining camps were built, chaotic in plan, with "no apparent beginning or end, congruity, or regard for the eternal fitness of things." Though most soon perished, some lived on to become respectable cities in their middle age. In these, stalwart masonry masses replaced the banner-fronted flimsy wooden shacks of the hurly-burly days, while Main Street still followed the course of the path picked out by the placer miners as they roamed frantically through town in search of a lead.

HOMESTEADING

In the 1820s and 1830s, a mere trickle of roving explorers, priests, fur trappers, hunters and Indian traders forayed into the western wilderness. During the course of the next three or four decades their faint trails were widened and rutted by the wagon wheels of settlers who sought to farm the land and make the West their home. Straggling westward homesteaders converged on Independence for the beginning of the long overland caravan trails. The Santa Fe Trail passed through Kansas and continued through Colorado to New Mexico. The Oregon Trail penetrated the settled lands of eastern Kansas and stretched north and west along the Platte River and through the territories of Nebraska and Montana.

Genoa, Nevada, circa 1870
Nevada Historical Society

Genoa, credited with being the oldest permanent settlement in Nevada, began as a Mormon trading post about 1850 in what was then part of the western Utah Territory. In 1857, the Mormons, forced to consolidate their holdings under pressure from U.S. troops, withdrew from the settlement. The Odd Fellows are posed in front of their meeting rooms.

Dallas, Oregon, circa 1860
Mill Street at Main
Polk County Historical Society

The protection from sun offered by trees in the East was generally provided by wooden porches in the West. Founded by transplanted New Englanders in 1851, Dallas was a gridiron town centered around a courthouse square.

In Idaho the trail divided, one branch heading north along the Snake River and through the Blue Mountains of Oregon to Astoria at the mouth of the Columbia River; the other, known as the California Trail, leading south through the Donner Pass to the Sacramento River Valley. Guarding the frontier was a chain of army posts extending from Fort Scott in Kansas, Fort Riley, Fort Kearney, Fort Laramie, Fort Hall, to Fort Walla Walla in the far Northwest.

By the end of the 1840s, in response to some irresistible force, like a magnet to its pole, or water to its level, Americans had expanded across the breadth of the continent. The nation's territory increased by nearly one third in that single decade: Texas was annexed; the Orgeon Treaty gave the nation undisputed claim to a vast area in the Pacific Northwest; from the Mexico Cession was created the state of California and the territories of Nevada, Utah and New Mexico.

The migrants moved in huge caravans—as foreigners in a strange land, for safety against the Indians, and for comfort against the harshness of the journey. Among them were dozens of groups which sought to establish colonies that would perpetuate their unique ethnic, religious or social patterns: abolitionist societies, temperance societies, and the

Sitka, Alaska
Alaska Historical Library

Founded as a Russian colony in 1799, Sitka was the site, in 1867, of the formal transfer of Russian America to United States ownership. A curious Indian-Russian-American hybrid, the town flourished as a fishing center.

San Juan Capistrano, 1900–1902
View south from mission
Charles Puck; Title Insurance and Trust Co.

The mission founded by Father Junípero
Serra in 1776 was in ruins long before this
photograph was taken. The wall running to
the right is that of the mission vineyard, while
the one at the left is the remains of the old
mission barracks. In the background, commercial buildings surround the plaza.

San Antonio, Texas, circa 1875
Main Street—Commerce Street
E. A. Doerr; Richard Russack Collection

The Spanish flavor in San Antonio—the most
important Spanish settlement in Texas—
persisted long after Texas became part of
the Union. Typically Spanish is rubblestone
construction, smoothed on the façade with
adobe cement.

communist society of the Community of True Inspiration;
Quakers, Mormons, Swiss River Brethren and Russian Men-
nonites; Swedes, Norwegians, Irish, Germans and others. The
Germans planted "Main Street" towns from Texas to California, in plan recalling the linear villages of their native land.
The "Oregon Fever" of the early 1840s brought to the Wil-
lamette Valley Congregationalists and Baptists from New
England, Ohio and Kentucky. The huge Mormon migration
brought to its City of Zion in the desert more than eight
thousand adherents in 1849, its first year.

While Indians roamed the northern Great Plains, in the
West and Southwest overland settlers came upon towns that
had long histories as French, Spanish or Indian settlements.
These towns grew as unique hybrid communities in which old
traditions flavored the new. The railroad engineer William
Bell described one of them: "It consists of a main street
lined on either side by adobe houses of one story with flat
roofs and few rooms. Many of these were stores belonging to
American traders, and were well-stocked with goods; two of
them were billiard saloons and two were boarding-houses
—all American innovations. There was no public house

Napoleonville, Louisiana, circa 1880
Avery Library, Columbia University

Located midway between Baton Rouge and
New Orleans, Napoleonville thrived as a
market community from the early nineteenth
century. A structure such as the drugstore of
M. Gouaux, with its steep hipped roof, reveals the village's French heritage.

proper, but strong drinks were sold at every one of these
establishments, and so far as I could make out, at every house
in town." In an Arizona town, a cluster of Indian adobe dwellings became the busy Main Street at a stagecoach terminal.
And from the sleepy plaza in the pueblo of Los Angeles in
Southern California, Main Street led to the huge Spanish-
held ranchos in the countryside.

The westward movement gathered momentum rapidly.
More western land—225 million acres—was settled and placed
under cultivation in the generation following the Civil War
than the total American land settled in the two centuries
preceding it. Much of the impetus for expansion of the agricultural frontier was the promise of free land given by the
Homestead Act of 1862. Once-barren land of the northern
plains became profitable wheat fields after the development
of grains that could weather the harsh dryness of prairie
winters, and through the technology developed in the last
quarter of the nineteenth century, including barbed-wire
fencing, reapers, steel plows, binders and steam-driven
threshers. Extensive acreage was needed to make such operation profitable. Under these circumstances, towns grew up at
great distances from one another; many could boast little
more than a Main Street.

Los Angeles, California, circa 1870
Main Street
Richard Russack Collection

Its exuberantly towered hotel gives Los Angeles's Main Street a distinctive
Spanish flavor.

39

Topeka, Kansas, 1876
Kansas Avenue
Leonard and Martin; Kansas State
Historical Society, Topeka

Scarcely twenty years old when this
photograph was taken for a local
business directory, Topeka had already achieved a substantial
appearance. Note the outsized
graphics, useful aid in such a
youthful community.

*Jordan Valley, Idaho,
circa 1912–1920
Blackaby's company store on
Main Street*
Otto M. Jones; Library of Congress

In the remote ranch country of
southwestern Idaho, Main Street
was little changed from home-
steading days through the First
World War era. Note the twentieth-
century material—corrugated metal
—used in the construction of the
building on the right.

*Ellsworth, Kansas, 1867
Walnut Street*
Alexander Gardner; Kansas State
Historical Society, Topeka

As the railroad moved west, the
cattle trail stretched east to join
it. Founded in 1867 beside the rails
of the Union Pacific, Ellsworth was
only a few months old at the time
of this photo.

42

CATTLE

After the Civil War, the trails of westward-moving pioneers were crossed by the wide swath of the Long Trail, cut by the hoofs of Texas longhorn cattle driving north. At first, the trail went only as far as the terminus of the railroad in Kansas, where cattle were penned until their purchase and shipment to eastern markets. Abilene, Wichita, Dodge City, Hays and Ellsworth were some of the "cow towns" whose Main Street, meeting the trail, was brought raucously to life by cowboys, cattle kings, soldiers and "bad men." Few structures were needed to serve the special needs of towns such as these. "The houses here are alternately Beer Houses, Whiskey Shops, Gambling Houses, Dance Houses and Restaurants," one reporter wrote. "There is little difference however, as the Beer Houses sell whiskey, and the whiskey houses retail beer." But where the economy of the cow towns diversified to include marketing, agricultural processing or the manufacture of farm machinery, the settlement took on a more permanent aspect. Brick and stone commercial buildings supplanted the porch-fronted saloons and dance halls. The trail was narrowed to accommodate the brick or plank sidewalks that provided pedestrian space. In one community, at least, the townspeople, resentful of the periodic invasion of the trail riders, even went so far as to block off the trail altogether.

The days of the Kansas cow towns were over by the 1870s. Cattle were now profitably grazed on the open grasslands farther north, where owners could bide their time in striking a bargain with eastern dealers. In the Dakotas, Wyoming, Montana, Idaho, Oregon and Washington, the old cow towns became trade and distribution centers serving back-country ranches. In these remote outposts, urban forms were reduced and simplified to the point of abstraction. "False fronts" conceal a jagged silhouette of pointed gables, and echo the flat roof lines of far-distant Main Street.

Rufus, Oregon, circa 1880
Main Street
W. A. Raymond; The Bettmann Archive

4. Depot

The industrialization of the East and the expansion of the West, inextricably linked, were the events that dominated nineteenth-century America. The widespread adoption of steam power in the 1840s and 1850s, for both railroad and factory, effected a profound transformation in the character of New England, from an agricultural and maritime economy to one based on commerce and industry.

In the first century of settlement, the gristmill stood alone near a waterfall. In the late eighteenth or early nineteenth century, a mill site on the river determined the location of a new grid town. But in the second half of the nineteenth century, steam-powered factories generated novel patterns of land use within existing towns. Freed from a stationary power source, these massive new structures could be built near the center of towns large enough to house a substantial labor force. Ambitious sons or daughters, impatient with their meager existence on subsistence farms, were drawn to these towns by the fresh opportunity. Here, also, flocked the landless Irish, English, Scottish and German immigrants who flooded the Northeast after the midcentury.

Some new industrial cities were founded in the East, but generally established towns and villages, peacefully self-contained for a century or two, were now transformed into manufacturing and commercial centers. Among these were Yonkers and Troy in New York, Waterbury and Torrington in Connecticut, Worcester, Fall River and Springfield in Massachusetts, Keene in New Hampshire, Pawtucket in Rhode

Independence, Iowa, circa 1875
Ensminge Brothers; International Museum of
Photography at George Eastman House

Independence was founded in 1847, its
town grid laid out along the banks of the
Wapsipinicon River. In the background, an
iron bridge spans the river, with a four-
story water-powered mill beside it.

Marlboro, Massachusetts, circa 1880
Shoe Factory of Boyd, Corey & Co.
Marlboro, Illustrated
Avery Library, Columbia University

Incorporated in 1660, Marlboro was an agricultural community for nearly two centuries
before rising to prominence as a leading
center for shoe production in the Civil War
period. In a scale to overwhelm the existing
streetscape, this huge mansard-roofed factory was built at the east end of Main Street.

Keene, New Hampshire, circa 1870
View from Unitarian Church tower
French and Sawyer; International Museum of Photography at
George Eastman House

Permanent settlement began in Keene about 1750. Its central square was
sited between Beaver Brook and the Ashuelot River, by whose side wool
milling began as early as 1815. By the second half of the nineteenth century,
the mill's tall smoking chimney was a landmark to rival the Congregational
Church tower, seen here at the left.

47

*Holyoke, Massachusetts,
circa 1875
Main Street, Dwight Street and
depot from Depot Hill*
George Ireland and Co.;
Richard Russack Collection

Holyoke was planned as a company town in 1847, to be served by
both railroad and river. But growth
lagged and it was only after the
1870s that the town was successful
as a manufacturing center. Main
Street shops carry the details of
that era's style, with flat or mansard
roofs and fancy window caps and
lintels.

Island, Portland in Maine. By the end of the Civil War, scores
of old village centers in New England and the Middle States
were encapsulated by concentric growth rings. Outlying
areas, many times larger than the original town, were incorporated within municipal limits. Districts of dark three-story
brick or frame tenements climbed over nearby fields where
corn or lettuce grew only the year before. Where once a tall
church spire dominated the vista, a massive factory chimney
spread a sooty haze over Main Street.

In the years following the Civil War, many an old town
center was transformed into "downtown." Specialized commercial and civic structures reflected the social and economic
complexities of the industrial age, modishly glorifying growth
and change. Courthouses, town halls, public libraries, graded

Pawtucket, Rhode Island, circa 1885
Main Street and square, looking west
Culver Pictures

A jagged skyline tells of Pawtucket's long history.

Worcester, Massachusetts, circa 1880
Main Street, Lincoln Square and
Lincoln Street
Worcester Historical Society

First the Blackstoné Canal and then a rail network were vital in making Worcester the nation's greatest industrial city not located on a natural waterway. Wire manufacture—one of Worcester's earliest industries and eventually her largest—was among the industries active in the Lincoln Square area at the north end of Main Street.

South Royalton, Vermont, 1901
Main Street and square
Culver Pictures

Across the green, the depot confronts the village church.

49

Buffalo, New York, 1902
Main Street
G. F. H. Bartlett; Buffalo and Erie County
Historical Society

The Mohawk and Edisonia hotels, at the left
of the photograph, record Buffalo's history
as a Great Lake port at the head of the Erie
Canal. The 1860s Tifft House marks the
beginning of Buffalo's railroad era, when the
city grew as a center second only to Chicago. At the time of this photograph, that
hotel is about to be demolished (note the
sign), for still another phase in Buffalo's
rapid development is under way; with the
newly harnessed power of Niagara Falls,
the city will rise to industrial prominence.
By the 1890s, heavy traffic necessitated
grade separation of railroad tracks.

schools, department stores and office buildings in brick,
granite and brownstone dwarfed the older frame structures
that stubbornly survived around them. Prominent at the far
end of Main Street—or on a hill high above it—were the
mansions of newly rich entrepreneurs for all to see, proof of
the town's success.

The railroad network expanded with industrialization. By
the eve of the Civil War, more than thirty thousand miles of
track fanned through the eastern hinterlands to agricultural
trading towns as far west as Iowa, Missouri, Arkansas and
Texas, and north to the lumber towns of Wisconsin and
Maine. Here was a ready market for the industrial products
of eastern factories. In the river valleys of the Kennebec,
Merrimack, Housatonic, Connecticut, Mohawk, Hudson,

Delaware and Susquehanna, railroad lines generally followed the course of the rivers and established roads, so traditional town centers retained their importance. The depot stayed near Main Street, though time and growth created a new hierarchy of spaces and structures.

The population of the larger towns and cities grew by leaps and bounds during the 1880s and 1890s. Growth and renewal transformed even well-established towns. "It is a very wonderful town, indeed, and it is not finished yet," Mark Twain said of St. Paul in *Life on the Mississippi.* "All the streets are obstructed with building material, and this is being compacted into houses as fast as possible, to make room for more—for other people are anxious to build, as soon as they can get the use of the streets to pile up their brick and stuff in."

A suburban fringe developed on city outskirts as commuter railroads carried workers to picturesquely styled new depots in old villages or neat new suburban towns, twenty,

Plymouth, New Hampshire, 1908
Main Street
Detroit Publishing Company;
Library of Congress

Ample in size and set well back from the sidewalk, post–Civil War dwellings—even on Main Street—reflect the suburban ideal.

51

thirty or forty miles from the city center. As towns thus blurred into the countryside, city-dwellers glanced longingly at unspoiled areas even farther away. Long-forgotten towns in such places as the Hudson highlands and the hills of western Massachusetts and Connecticut were discovered by prosperous merchants, who sent real estate prices skyrocketing in response to their demand for bucolic weekend or summer retreats. Some sought quiet escape to the southlands. Architect Louis Sullivan recalls a boyhood journey to the Mississippi Gulf Coast: "With daylight, there revealed itself an undulating village . . . a village sleeping out as it had slept for generations with untroubled surface . . . the general store, the post office, the barber shop, the meat market on Main Street, sheltered by ancient live oaks, the saloon near the depot. . . ."

Grand resort towns were laid out in scenic locations from Florida to Maine and as far west as the mountains of Colorado and the southern California oases. Prosperous middle-class vacationers crowded the broad verandas of the splendid hotels that lined the wide and shaded Main Street. More rustic were the picturesque campsites built by the Methodist Meetings at the seashore or deep in the woods.

In the South, until the coming of the railroad, towns were few, and cities still fewer. "Nothing is more evident than the fact, that our people have never entertained a proper opinion of the importance of home cities. Blindly, and greatly to our own injury, we have contributed hundreds of millions of dollars toward the erection of mammoth cities in the North, while our own magnificent bays and harbors have been most shamefully neglected," chided the southerner Hinton Helper. Too late in history to undermine the devastating social and economic institution of the plantation system, which scattered and isolated the population of the South, the process of urbanization was finally begun as the railroads penetrated remote inland regions in the 1840s and 1850s. On the eve of the Civil War, the South had nine thousand miles of railroads, a network comparable to other sections of the country, and there was through-rail connection from New York to New Orleans. Amid vast stretches of pine forests and sand barrens, station villages were at first little more than a mean

Saratoga Springs, New York, 1889
Broadway
Seneca Roy Stoddard; Library of Congress

Broad and shaded, this main street is a fine
site for a promenade. The town began as a
spa in the early nineteenth century, though
its grand hotels date from the Civil War
period, when horse breeding and racing
were magnets for tourists.

Coronado Tent City, Coronado Beach
California, circa 1902
Detroit Publishing Company;
Library of Congress

Framing the vista of this tent city Main Street
is the grand hotel, built in 1888 (at a reputed
cost of a million dollars) by the Coronado
Beach Company, developers of this ambitious resort scheme.

Mobile, Alabama, 1894
Front Street
Art Work of Mobile and Vicinity,
W. H. Parish Publishing Company
Avery Library, Columbia University

Cotton, lumber and, in the last decades of
the nineteenth century, iron and steel were
the chief products shipped from Mobile,
Alabama's single port. As in many river
cities, a specialized wholesale main street
developed along the riverfront and the railroad tracks that paralleled it.
Cast-iron balconies, decorative at the upper
stories, utilitarian at the working level, are
characteristic of the region and the period.

53

Colorado Springs, Colorado, circa 1900
Pikes Peak Avenue
William Henry Jackson; State Historical
Society of Colorado

Colorado Springs, a speculative development along the line of the Denver and Rio
Grande Railroad, was well provided with
amenities. Not the least of these was the
judicious siting of the main street, Pikes
Peak Avenue, to capture the drama of the
mountain that gave the street its name.

Atlanta, Georgia, 1872
Peachtree Street
Atlanta Historical Society

First known by the name of Terminus,
Atlanta came into being in 1837 as a stop at
the end of the railroad line. During the Civil
War, Atlanta's strategic location made it the
transportation capital of the Confederacy.

huddle of dirty white frame houses along the railroad tracks.
Towns were often laid out without benefit of a survey at all;
their limits were simply defined by a radius from the depot.
County seats, though patterned on the grid, were distinctly
southern in character. "Warsaw, Benton County, Missouri, is
a genuine southern town, surrounding a hollow square with a
court-house in the center," wrote the journalist A. D. Richardson. "Streets gullied by water and overgrown with weeds;
frame houses, log houses and stucco houses, with deep
porticos and shade trees; negros trudging with burdens on
their backs; deserted buildings; tumbling fences and a
genuine tendency to the 'demnition bow wows.'"

But, slowly, the railroad had its impact on the South. The
lumber, coal and iron industries hastened the growth of
towns in Tennessee, Alabama and Mississippi. The processing
of tobacco in Virginia and the collection and manufacture of
cotton in Georgia and the Carolinas gave birth to new inland
towns which united the railway with the long-used river network.

In the West, the railroad was the precursor of civilization.

"Before the census of 1860 shall be printed, the whistle of the locomotive and the roar of the rolling train will be heard at nearly every house and hamlet of the wide central plain, and no one but a hermit will be living beyond the cheering sound these will give forth," boasted Jessup W. Scott, who was both a newspaperman and a land speculator. Travelers to the midwestern prairies were thrilled by the vastness of the space which unfolded before them. They found a "pre-ordained fitness between the railroad and the prairie," and they exulted in the conquering power of the steam engine. The last of the frontier east of the Mississippi was put to the plow when tracks reached Illinois, Indiana and Wisconsin in the 1850s. Where streams of caravans had crossed the prairie, now boxcars brought the new immigrants to farm and to fill its towns, supplied fuel and equipment, and returned with agricultural products for eastern markets.

Although speculators played an important part in the development of western towns, there is little doubt that the railroad was the greatest town builder of all. The Illinois Central Railroad, chartered in 1851, was the first land grant railroad. In less than six years, more than seven hundred miles of track were laid in Illinois to connect it with the South and West. In wholesale fashion, dozens of grid towns were planted along its path. At the site of the depot there grew a town. The suc-

Centralia, Illinois
Looking west across tracks from north side
of passenger station
Illinois State Historical Library

Centralia was one of thirty-three speculative towns developed along the line of the Illinois Central. Each town followed a standard plat and had identical street names and numbers.

Sacramento, California, circa 1870
Front Street
A. J. Russell; Oakland Museum History
Department

Sacramento grew as a river port during the
gold rush and as a rail center when the
mining frontier moved east.

cess of the Illinois Central established a precedent for making
huge land grants to promote rapid rail construction and
town-building. Towns along the routes of the Kansas Pacific,
Denver Pacific, Northern Pacific, Santa Fe and Great Northern were similarly developed.

Aggressive railroad promotional campaigns lured population to western towns. "Before the flowers bloom another
year, Dakota will have her railroads," a propagandist
promised in 1870. "Towns and cities will spring into existence, and the steam whistle and the noise of saws and hammers and the clack and clatter of machinery, the sound of
industry will be heard." Railways were eager to sell their
town lots and to create a demand for the alternate sections
which they had been granted along the right of way.

The drama of rail construction was intense. There had
been talk of a transcontinental rail link since the 1850s, but
construction began only in 1865. The lands of the "Great
American Desert" were harsh, the dangers unknown, the
distance enormous. Yet the speed with which tracks crossed
the nation was remarkable. From Omaha, Nebraska, the line

was pushed westward by the Union Pacific, while it was sent eastward from Sacramento, California, by the Central Pacific. As construction proceeded, impromptu towns mushroomed at the end of the line; these consisted of little more than a Main Street with a depot and a few beer halls and gambling saloons to serve the construction crews. A couple of months later, as the tracks stretched into the distance, the motley structures were picked up by the departing workers and deposited at the new railhead farther along, leaving behind only the name and a patch of bare earth.

One of the last of the great land booms occurred in California when the lines of the Santa Fe and the Southern Pacific met in Los Angeles in 1885. H. Ellington Brooks, a California historian, chronicled the events a few years later: "After that

Grants Pass, Oregon, 1910
Main Street, looking west
Oregon Historical Society

it is difficult to follow the course of the boom, so rapid and immense was the advance. People poured in by the thousands and prices of land climbed rapidly. Everybody that could find an office went into the real-estate business, either as agents, as speculators, or as operators. Tracts of land by the score were cut into lots. Auctions, accompanied by brass bands and free lunches, drew their crowds. At private sales lines were formed, before daybreak, in front of the seller's office, for fear there would not be enough lots to go around." Fortunes rose or fell according to the direction taken by the tracks. Speculation in town sites and city lots was rampant; the success of a town was assured if and only if a railroad went through it. The town passed by had few alternatives: to scheme for a spur to connect with a major line; to pick up, lock, stock, and barrel, and move to a site favored by the railroad; or to resign itself to a steady decline.

TWO

STRUCTURE

5. Form and Order

Main Street was the face of a town, the expression of its identity. The form of each Main Street was a unique configuration: buildings of every size and shape; a skyline silhouette; built forms and open spaces; the rhythm of windows and walls; the texture of wood, iron, glass and masonry; the contours of pediment, cornice, lintel and carved bracket; the shadow of church tower or signpost.

Historic patterns of transportation determined if Main Street was a level site along a canal or a hill sloping down to railroad tracks. The influence of climate and geography was significant: prairie towns were bare and wind-swept; rows of pride-of-India trees formed shady passages in Georgia; elms and oaks were graceful arches over Connecticut Main Streets.

Even if it was no more than a dozen facing structures across a wide space, Main Street was a magnet for human activity. Residential, religious, civic, educational, recreational, commercial and ceremonial use took place side by side. Through the first part of the nineteenth century, structures tended to be multifunctional: the church basement held the general store or shoemaker; the carpenter (also the undertaker) lived above or behind his store; the schoolhouse was the library and public meeting place. Specialization increased the number of structures, but diminished the extent of their utilization. Meeting house yielded to church, town hall, academy, police station, lodge hall, opera house and movie theater. Domestic parlors gave way to ice cream parlors, shoeshine parlors, tonsorial parlors, beauty parlors, billiard parlors and funeral parlors. The general store and the one-room doctor's or lawyer's office was supplanted by differentiated establishments which vended an increasingly large number of goods and services. Some forms disappeared altogether, and new ones took their place. Improved food-preservation technology virtually eliminated the market house, but permitted the luncheonette; the blacksmith and livery gave way to the automobile showroom, gas station and used-car lot; the hotel on the town square yielded to the motel on the "strip." The village green was paved for parking space; new uses were found even for the graveyard.

In one town after another, almost without regard to region or period or community resources, certain elements came to symbolize Main Street structures: the tall church spire; the town hall cupola; the carved and molded bank door; the fancy date numerals inscribed on the pedimented commercial block; the pillared hotel veranda. Time-honored street-level symbols were the barbershop pole, the jeweler's clock, the cigar store Indian. New activities generated still others—the soda fountain's Coca-Cola sign, the movie marquee, the gas station's motley string of plastic pennants.

Local tradition played its part in building the streetscape. A Spanish heritage left its legacy in arcaded structures along a plaza; an English past bequeathed the row house; towns derived from the Philadelphia type generally emphasized both the vertical and the horizontal axis. Local or regional idiom was closely related to indigenous materials and the availability of native artisans skilled in using them. Building scale, proportion and decorative detail responded to the use of timber in Oregon, Wisconsin or Connecticut, granite in Maine or Massachusetts, adobe clay in the Southwest, field-stone in the Hudson River Valley or Pennsylvania, limestone in Kansas or Michigan. Moreover, local construction techniques often persisted even after building façades were given more modish treatment.

With the professionalization of architectural practice after the mid nineteenth century, the ability of the architect to influence the field was enhanced. Local craftsmen adapted new styles enthusiastically as examples were illustrated in plan books and periodicals. These largely supplanted the heavily

Changing styles of Commercial Architecture

Changing Main Street style is seen best in commercial structures. These are more numerous than public buildings and generally have a shorter life span. The renderings below—from the collection of the Avery Library, Columbia University—were published in architectural books and periodicals between 1856 and 1916. Architect-designed structures—though more sophisticated than the works of the builder-contractor—were the inspiration that kept Main Street in style.

Design for six stores
Ranlett, *City Architecture,* 1856

This commercial row of the 1850s continues the tradition of the warehouse, store and row house of the 1820s and 1830s. The block is composed of a series of three-bay units, essentially domestic in scale. Heavy, closely spaced supports at the ground story limit the size of window openings. Ornamental balcony and stair railings, no doubt intended to be cast iron, and the patterned brickwork beneath the cornice, are restrained embellishments to the sober design of the façade.

65

*Design for People's Bank, Wheeling,
West Virginia*
S. M. Howard, in *American Architect and
Building News,* March 27, 1876

In the post–Civil War period, the grand
palazzo—deliberately recalling the mercantile glory of the Italian Renaissance—
was a favorite mode for bank and insurance
office. Hallmarks of the style are: rhythmically
spaced round and segmentally arched window openings, projecting cornice and dated
pediment supported on elaborate brackets,
rusticated and carved stone, rich moldings
and sculptural detailing.

*A block of stores with apartments connected
Saratoga Springs, New York*
C. B. Croff, in *Progressive Architecture,* 1875

Adapted to the commercial row, the *palazzo*
style enjoyed great popularity during the
Gilded Age, although the design was greatly
simplified and based on repeating units.
(Note the alternation of two-window and
three-window bays on the Saratoga façades.)
Ponderous masonry at the first story gives
way to large plate-glass display windows,
usually framed by cast-iron members.
Molded iron, stamped sheet metal or
machine-carved wood is fashioned in intricate forms for column, pier, capital, lintel
and cornice. The façade is unified by an
arched pediment in the center, which is
echoed by smaller arches at the ends of the
building. Finials punctuate the horizontal roof
line. The style of street architecture should
be rich, the critics wrote, for splendid buildings not only delight the eye, but are "the
perpetual paean of a marvelous mercantile
success."

Design for building on Main Street, Worcester, Massachusetts
S. C. Earle and J. E. Fuller, in *American Architect and Building News*, April 1, 1876

The French Second Empire version of the palazzo style favors the mansard roof—which minimizes an awkwardly high fifth story—and emphasizes variety and individuality in shape, material and color. On the Worcester building, note the varied window groupings and the alternation of Tudor arch and lancet arch openings.

Design for Orange Music Hall, Orange, New Jersey
Silliman and Farnsworth, in *American Architect and Building News*, August 28, 1880

Opera house and music hall are often exuberantly styled. Note the bold treatment of the piers flanking the entrance to the Orange Music Hall, the sculptural richness of its façade and the flamboyant silhouette of its roof line. At the same time, the plan is soberly practical, efficiently combining space for entertainment, municipal services, office and shop. A recessed shop entrance permits display windows.
Canvas canopies, a welcome amenity for the pedestrian, complement the billowing forms of the late-Victorian design.

ORANGE MUSIC HALL
ORANGE, N.J.
SILLIMAN & FARNSWORTH
ARCHITECTS NEW YORK.

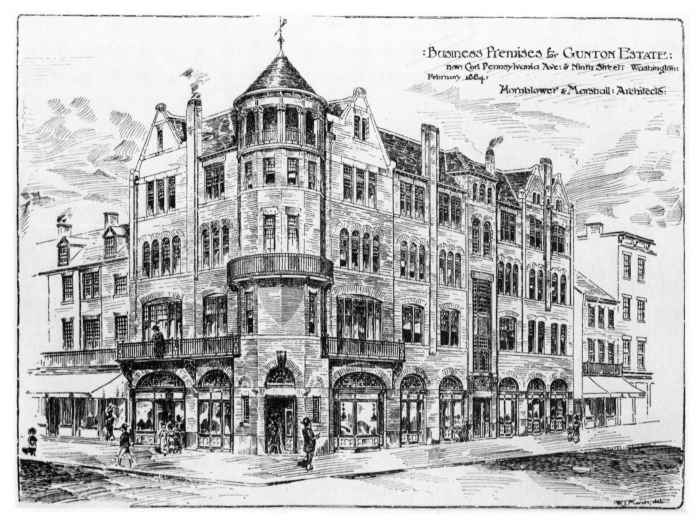

Design for business premises, Washington, D.C.
Hornblower and Marshall, in *American Architect and Building News,*
December 13, 1884

The highly individualistic Romanesque Revival style was popular through
the 1880s. The architect of the Washington block unabashedly ignores the
norms of the street with regard to roof line, number and height of stories,
rhythm of windows and treatment of display windows. In fact, the window
treatment seems altogether idiosyncratic: note that the windows are vari-
ously shaped and sized and appear singly, or grouped in twos, threes, fours
or fives. Wall dormers, corner turret and dark-hued masonry are also characteristic of the style.

Design for bank and office building, Nashville, Tennessee (opposite)
Thompson and Cibel, in *American Architect and Building News,*
May 31, 1890

By the 1890s, a classicizing trend was under way. Column, pilaster, pediment, arch, urn and festoon were part of the classical vocabulary employed
to reduce the monotony of seemingly endless ranges of window openings on
tall buildings. Elaborate horizontal coursing at the second, third, fourth and
sixth stories is used to enliven this façade, to reduce its apparent height and
to visually relate the building to its neighbors. A heavy projecting cornice,
supported by elaborate brackets and surmounted by an ornate balustrade,
effectively crowns the eighth story. In this period, the exterior becomes but
a masonry shell, enclosing a self-supporting interior steel skeleton. Light-
toned brick or masonry was preferred.

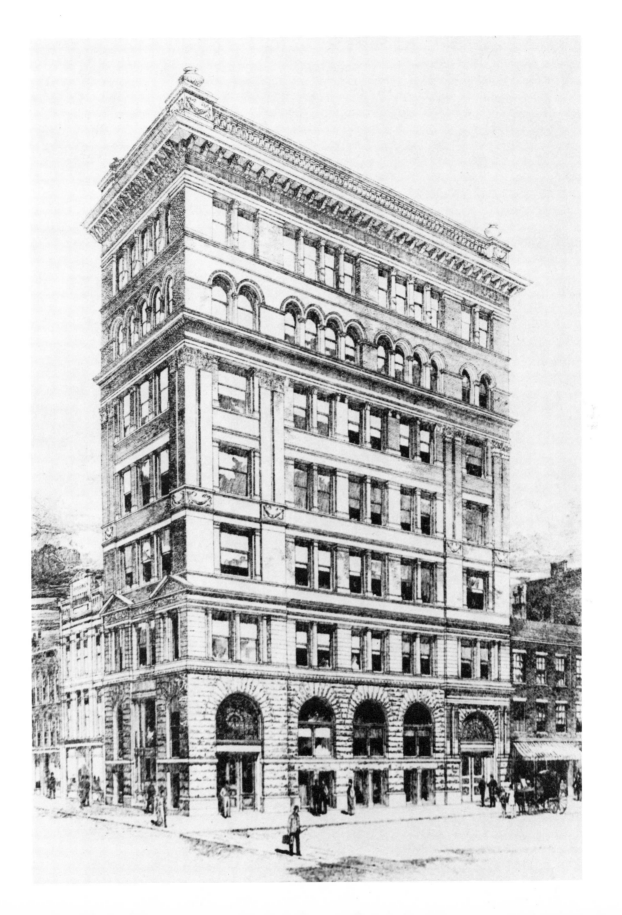

Design for Merchants National Bank, New Bedford, Massachusetts
Chapman and Frazer, in *American Architect and Building News,*
January 27, 1894

In the spirit of the Beaux Arts Renaissance, which dominated the years after
the 1893 Chicago Columbian Exposition, the bank exudes a somewhat self-
conscious dignity. But there is grandeur in the cadence of the window openings and the impressive stone piers between the display windows, elegance
in the sconces flanking the doorways and the richly ornamented cornice,
simplicity in the restrained detailing and the integrated designs for signs.
The "City Beautiful" bank continued to be popular for decades. A pair of
Ionic columns and, site permitting, a rounded corner were favorite motives.

Land and Loan Office, Algona, Iowa
Louis H. Sullivan, in *The Architectural
Record,* May, 1916

The buildings of Louis Sullivan (and his
few followers) were brilliant additions to
some midwestern Main Street corners.
Highly personal and frankly modern were
Sullivan's solutions to the design problems
of the small-town corner commercial building: how to create a dramatic entrance;
how to differentiate front and sides; how
to use ornament; how to relate to existing
buildings.

Design for Seneca Building, Buffalo, New York
McKenzie, Voorhees and Gmelin, in *Architecture and Building,* August 1912

In the World War I era, the tall building, expressively vertical (note the projecting ribs on the Seneca Building), rose as a sheer tower fifteen stories or more. Despite its advanced technology, this skyscraper relies on historical details: moldings, ornament, gabled dormers, and cupolas. After the war, zoning was commonly used to reduce building bulk by requiring setbacks at the upper stories. Not until the post–World War II building boom did the skyscraper emerge as an unadorned slab.

used builders' handbooks which, reprinted with few changes year after year, had been the support of the vernacular and often highly individual interpretations of classic Greek and Roman forms that had constituted the architectural vocabulary for more than a century. For the post–Civil War generation, the availability of plans, elevations and specifications enabled even the smallest town or village to don its own version of any of a number of modish Victorian garbs. As architectural canon was diffused, new technologies developed and the national transportation network improved—wood, masonry, metal, glass and other materials were commonly transported over vast distances to make up for local shortages or to conform to current style. Vermont slate, sandstone from the Hudson Palisades or Ohio, Tennessee marble and California cedar, for example, were among a host of materials that built Main Streets many hundreds of miles from their quarries, factories or millyards.

In eastern towns founded in the seventeenth or eighteenth century, and even in nineteenth-century western towns, the scale of Main Street was comfortably related to its users. Common construction techniques—complete timber framing, or masonry bearing walls carrying an interior wooden framework—limited building size. Window, doorway and ornament related monuments like the church or town hall to the scale of the single dwelling unit. The narrow and deep building lot —commonly 25 to 30 feet in width and 125 to 150 feet in depth—was a size that demonstrated distinct advantages for commercial use on emerging Main Streets; purchase was easily accomplished by a small entrepreneur, construction was rapid and economical, and a densely built Main Street offered the users considerable convenience.

At first, Main Street structures were hardly deeper than wide. When greater size was needed, as purchase power and the taste for luxury grew, their length came to occupy nearly the full depth of their lot, crowding out incidental users, like the barbershop, the lumberyard or the livery stable. Until the 1850s, height was limited to two or three stories. About the time of the Civil War, building height commonly shot up to four or even five stories, the greatest practical height until the widespread use of the elevator in the early twentieth century made space on upper stories as desirable as on street level. But if buildings couldn't get higher at first, they did become larger. And in the building boom of the late 1860s to early 1870s and then again in a second boom in the late 1880s and early 1890s, the taste was for grand scale. The commercial block which first achieved popularity in the Civil War years achieved its richest and fullest expression in the closing decade of the nineteenth century. Four, five or six lots, and eventually as much as a total square block, were combined to form a single architectural statement. Divided into individual bays or shopfronts, their street façade was often reminiscent of an earlier Main Street, while upper stories efficiently used the building as a single unit. Here were located clubrooms, a theater seating as many as a thousand patrons, a roller-skating rink, a business college or hotel. Methods and materials of the machine age—power tools, steel framing, waterproof roofing, plate glass, concrete blocks and machine-made bricks—aided the move toward bigness. On older Main Streets especially, shifts in scale were often dramatic. As the twentieth century opened, Main Street's skyline was exploded by a new architectural form, the tall office building. Intolerant of preindustrial relics, the creative energy of the new age resisted the constraints imposed by the traditional urban fabric.

In the brief span of American urbanization, the historical forces that built Main Street ordered its elements into a remarkably consistent pattern—a pattern that has been shattered only in our own era. From the New England coast to the California citrus fields, the image of Main Street was easy to conjure: a dominant axis within a grid; a transportation and communication artery; a familiar sequence of function and activity. Main Street was both a stopping place and a corridor, a pedestrian space and a through road. And Main Street thrived only as long as this equilibrium was maintained.

On youthful Main Streets, structures briefly held as their own the space in front occupied by veranda or covered platform, though in deference to urbanism they ultimately yielded it to the space of the street, where a wooden or flagstone sidewalk regulated the building line and marked a continuous pedestrian zone. High interest and pleasurable social experience made this a place to linger: awnings and projecting cornices were shelters from rain; entrances were inviting; merchandise was appealing behind plate-glass windows; ornate iron fences set off trim churchyard lawns planted with colorful flower beds; dwellings were fronted by wicker-furnished porches. The roadway was used by wheeled vehicles, though until the automobile claimed it exclusively, this space was shared with pedestrians. Down the center, trolley tracks allowed rapid and efficient movement. On either side, a wide variety of carts, wagons and surreys was accommodated. Utility poles held a forest of wires that roofed the street. Curbstones marked off the street from the sidewalk; this interface also served as a sometime market and informal resting place. In older towns, or in more fortunate ones, the common or town square was nearby.

Signs and symbols—in communicating information about location, function and activity—helped to organize an increasingly complex urban environment. On Main Street there revived the venerable practice of embellishing architectural forms with painted and molded images and word symbols. Graphics, supergraphics, logos, emblems, pictorial devices, electric signs and other vernacular heraldry were emblazoned on the front, back and sides of Main Street structures. While at first display artists were limited to tin or cut-and-painted wood, ultimately they were able to perform exuberant experiments with an enormous variety of weather-resistant pigments, fabrics and metals.

A major intersection usually served as Main Street's focus —the vigorous expression of a nation on the move. The largest and most important civic or commercial structures were crowded nearby. Main Street's corners were particularly coveted, their use usually claimed by high-volume or high-prestige establishments, the drugstore or bank. The imposing mass or architectural eccentricity of corner buildings gave

Main Street signs

Main Street advertising—as American as the hot dog—has always been as aggressive as technology permitted. Blatant they are, these carved and gilded signatures, painted board and canvas placards, electric light boxes, supersized wall graphics and hung signs, steel space frame and neon-tube stabiles, but lively, too, preserving layers of time, displaying imagination and ingenuity, promising comfort, delight and fulfillment. The decline of the art occurred in the 1950s.

New London, Connecticut, circa 1860
Connecticut Historical Society

Cincinnati, Ohio, 1887
Cincinnati Historical Society

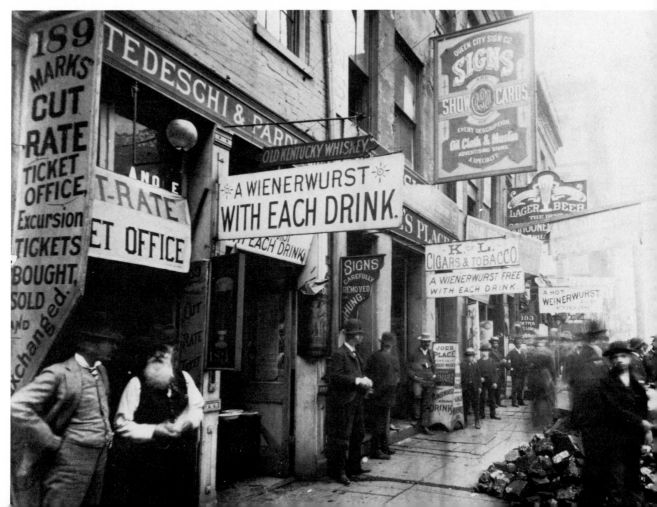

Buffalo, New York, circa 1900, Library of Congress

Minot, North Dakota, circa 1910
State Historical Society of Wisconsin

Delaware, Ohio, 1930
Library of Congress

Cascade, Iowa, 1937
Library of Congress

Albuquerque, New Mexico, circa 1955
Photoworld, Inc.

Memphis, Tennessee, circa 1960
Memphis Chamber of Commerce

Newport, Rhode Island, 1970
Cervin Robinson, Historic American
Buildings Survey

Baltimore, Maryland, 1970
Baltimore Department of Housing and
Community Development

weight to the intersection and provided a spatial scale for Main Street, marking off the single blocks along its length. While in larger towns and cities, cross streets became as densely built as Main Street itself, in smaller urban centers their space proved surprisingly shallow, quickly dwindling to an uneven assortment of one-story wooden shopfronts, artisans' workrooms and modest dwellings fronted by fenced or terraced gardens. In the East, Main Street began as omni-functional, but in the West, some degree of specialization took place from the beginning. School, town hall, courthouse, were often relegated to parallel or side streets.

Large shade trees marked upper Main Street; well into the twentieth century, this was the prestige residential section. Its dominant architectural style reflected the date of the town's greatest prosperity. Mills, storage depots or small industry usually took up the other end of the street, and the train station was there as well. Local custom varied the Main Street pattern in many ways: in strongly teetotaling communities, saloons could be found only on side streets; in most towns, the railroad tracks had a "right" and a "wrong" side; and in one western city, at least, the decent dwellings on the north side of Main Street primly regarded a row of brothels on the south side.

Youthful American towns achieved a remarkable specialization and Main Street spaces and structures revealed their differences: the string of supply shops and saloons in a mining town; the riverfront wall of mills and boardinghouses in a textile-manufacturing town; the cluster of inns and suppliers in a transit center on the western route; the dignified parade of mansions on the Main Street of a college town. Some towns changed function during the course of their history: Dallas was first a cotton town, later an oil distribution center; Nantucket prospered as a whaling center, and then as a resort. One Main Street, engulfed by suburbia, grows as a segment of a twelve-mile commercial strip. Another, abandoned by the railroad, can only wither and die.

Shaped by complex historical forces, the rigor of geography and climate, and the demands of function, Main Street is one moment, and many, in the flow of time. At any given point, a Main Street configuration was a unique response to myriad stimuli, a singular expression of time and place.

6. Time and Place

What follows is an attempt to capture some moments of the American environment, to glimpse the face of Main Street at different times, and in different places. The Main Streets of seven towns are documented through a series of photographs; for each town they are generally the work of a single local photographer. The earliest series is from the 1870s, the latest from the 1920s. Close "reading" reveals the richness of our environmental heritage in both its unity and its diversity, and provides an understanding of where we have been and, perhaps, of where we might be going.

That these seven Main Streets were uncovered, and not seven others, is partly the result of chance, and yet each Main Street has its own story to tell about its time, and its place.

Richmond, Virginia, shows the effect of the Civil War and postwar regeneration—although Chattanooga or Atlanta might have served equally well. In New England—though for different reasons and in a different way—Hartford's Main Street just as surely reflected profound changes in American urban life and form in the second half of the nineteenth century.

On the edge of the great prairie grew hundreds of agricultural towns; Junction City's plain limestone buildings bequeath a special legacy. Like other college towns, Geneva, New York, has a particular grace, but its forms were also influenced by other factors, such as the many southerners who settled there, and its position at the head of Seneca Lake.

The streetscape of Orange, New Jersey, reveals the gradual

suburbanization of a settlement whose roots are deep in colonial history. And in Stillwater, Minnesota, and Pendleton, Oregon, are glimpsed two of the more poignant episodes of the American past—the heedless exploitation of natural resources and the closing of the frontier. But the same story might have been told of Jerome, Arizona, or Fairbanks, Alaska.

Every Main Street has its own story to tell.

GENEVA, NEW YORK
A Saints' Retreat and Old Maids' Paradise

Child of an idealistic real estate developer, Main Street, Geneva, was born in the era of the turnpike. The developer, Captain Charles Williamson, was agent for the Pulteney Associates, a group of Englishmen who had in 1792 purchased a million and a half acres in western New York State. Williamson was fired a few years later; his enthusiasm to provide urban amenities as a lure for settlement in the western wilderness may have exceeded his business acumen. But Main Street flourished for a generation longer. It was dignified by an elegant hotel on its public square, built by Williamson at a substantial cost, a row of sophisticated town houses, handsome mansions, and an impressive array of churches and educational buildings. By the 1830s the town's population had climbed from a few hundred to more than three thousand, but the canal had triumphed over the turnpike and Main Street was left a· quiet backwater. Thus it remained through the nineteenth century; in the words of native son Warren Hunting Smith: "a citadel of culture in a commercial nation, a haven of leisure in a bustling world, and an oasis of Southerners in a land of Yankees."

Main Street intersected the path of the Genesee Turnpike, the land route from Albany to the west. From a north–south ridge, Main Street commanded a splendid view of Seneca Lake, one hundred feet below. Near the street's north end was the public square and the grand Geneva Hotel. Shops occupied the ground floors of elegant brick row houses surrounding the square, while their proprietors could live above. Geneva achieved importance as a stop on the stage route. Among the aristocratic Virginians lured to Geneva by reports of her fertile soil and salubrious atmosphere were John Nichols and Colonel Robert Selden Rose, who, respectively, purchased 1,600- and 1,200-acre farms on either side of Seneca Lake. They brought with them seventy-five slaves; freed in the early nineteenth century, they were the beginning of a permanent black community in Geneva.

Joining in cultivated social intercourse with southern Episcopalians and New England Presbyterians were the offspring of old Dutch Reform families of the Hudson River Valley, the Van Rensselaers, Schiefflins and Bogerts. Intermarriages resulted in a tight dynasty which reigned over Geneva from spacious Federal, Greek Revival and Gothic Revival Main Street mansions.

The year 1825 was epochal for Geneva, as it was for all New York State. That year the Erie Canal was opened, creating a through water route from the Great Lakes to the Hudson River and New York harbor, and signaling a new era of growth and prosperity. With the completion of the Cayuga and Seneca Canal a few years later, Geneva was able to share in the brisk canal trade. But it was the "Bottom," or the land along the lakefront, which was now the scene of commercial activity. On the "Hill" above, Main Street was left peaceful and unspoiled for exclusive use of residences and cultural, educational and religious institutions. Here was the fifteen-acre campus of Geneva (later Hobart) College, created in 1822 by the marriage of the old Geneva Academy with a central New York Episcopal seminary. The Geneva Medical College and Trinity Church, both built in 1841, were splendid Main Street embellishments. That same year, the public square was enclosed as a park and beautified by tree-planting. The lake side of Main Street, originally prohibited to construction so the view of the lake would remain unobstructed, was filled in with pleasant cottages. Older homes were carefully maintained and cautiously remodeled.

Through the balance of the canal era, Geneva prospered as the center of a nursery and tree-growing industry; there was never much reason to alter the face of Main Street. In the post–Civil War period, Geneva became something of an industrial center, specializing in the production of iron stoves, boilers and optical equipment. A network of railroad lines radiated from the town center. By 1898, Geneva's population reached ten thousand; the town was formally chartered as a city. Even at that late date, Main Street remained tightly held by old-time institutions: Hobart College, the churches, retired clergymen and the unmarried daughters of stubbornly surviving families. Retaining the leisurely charm of another era, Main Street was known as the "Saints' Retreat and the Old Maids' Paradise."

The photographs were taken in the decades of the 1870s and 1880s by photographer J. G. Vail and are in the collection of the Geneva Historical Society. They are arranged to suggest the sequence from Jay Street, at the southern end of Main Street, north to Castle Street Corners and the commercial heart of town.

Plan of Geneva, New York
A. Pomery & Co., Atlas of Ontario County, 1874
Geneva Historical Society

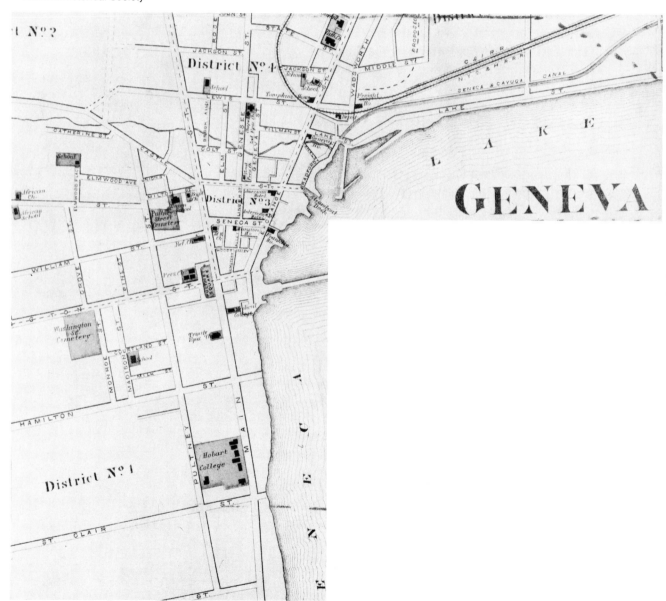

Stagecoach on Pulteney Street

View toward Main Street from Hamilton Street

Main Street is seen as little more than a shallow fringe with orchards and
fenced fields pushing up close behind it.
The view from Hamilton Street, past the Hobart College campus, to Pulteney
Park, takes in the churches of the Main Street elite: on the right, the Trinity
Episcopal; at the left, in the distance, the Presbyterian.

Trinity and Recitation halls, Hobart College

Dwellings, South Main Street

Geneva attained her first full flower in the
optimistic decade of the 1830s, apogee of
the Greek Revival style in western New
York. As on the building at the left, architectural elements from classical Greece
were used as symbols of that distant golden
age, which Americans hoped the present one
would rival. Particularly popular was the
columned portico; suggesting a temple front,
it also offered the practical advantage of a
covered veranda.

Trinity Church

Built in 1841, Trinity Church marks an early stage in Gothic Revival church architecture. This was a mode that, in one variation or another, dominated ecclesiastical, especially Episcopalian, architecture for the balance of the nineteenth century.

The dwelling at the right, with its lacy, carpenter-crafted ornament at eaves, balcony and portico, exemplifies the domestic version of the Gothic Revival style.

Pulteney Park

In the vanguard of developing civic consciousness, Geneva's Pulteney Square—part of Williamson's original town plan—was planted and set off as a park in 1841. Additional amenities were added in the 1870s, when Geneva joined the growing number of welfare-minded communities then forming Civic Improvement Associations.

Row houses facing Pulteney Park

Sophisticated row house architecture, something of an anomaly in the wide-open spaces of western New York in the late eighteenth and early nineteenth centuries, testified to Captain Williamson's appreciation for the urban ensembles of the South. The row house remained a popular type in Geneva as late as the 1860s and 1870s. While the plan changed little over the decades, increasingly decorative details at cornice, window and door opening record changing taste.

Commerce or craft was often carried on in the first story, while upper stories provided dwelling space. The passageway reveals a view of Seneca Lake.

91

Geneva waterfront on Seneca Lake, showing South Exchange Street, harbor, Nestor Malt House

Seneca Street, view west toward Main Street

Commercial structures lining Seneca Street were built between the 1830s, when the steamboat replaced the stagecoach, and the 1870s, when the railroad supplanted them both. From year to year changes were only slight, reflecting the conservatism of a relatively quiet agricultural backwater. At the head of Seneca Street is Main Street.

RICHMOND, VIRGINIA
Main Street Reborn in the Industrial Age

As the Civil War came to its weary end, the order was given to evacuate Richmond, the city which for four years had served as capital of the Confederacy. Starting in the warehouses along the James River, great fires lit the city as its population fled. Main Street was little more than a smoking rubble when Union troops took Richmond.

In digging out from the ruins of her past, Richmond's development, like that of cities in the North in the postwar era, was marked by enormous population increase, rapid industrialization and a profound disjuncture with historic patterns. In the 1870–1890 period, Richmond not only added to her corporate boundaries, but increased her population by 60 percent, to more than eighty thousand. The iron industry was the first to recover. In 1867, the vast Tredegar Army Iron Works, remembered by later historians as the "Krupp of the Confederacy," was one of more than a dozen factories back in operation. Tobacco processing and flour milling were not far behind. The residential quarters of town shifted to the north and west, bringing the retail trade district along with them. On Main Street there grew a money and wholesale merchandise market so specialized that each block seemed to claim a different use: banks, lawyers, real estate and insurance agents filled the 1000 block, across from the post office and custom house, and the 1100 block; commission agents and dry-goods merchants dominated the 1200 block; wholesale grocers, druggists and hardware merchants were grouped on the next two; dealers in plumbing and agricultural implements clustered on the 1500 block. Tobacco warehouses and iron foundries took title to the riverfront.

Though no insurance moneys were payable for losses sustained in the conflagration, these blocks on Main Street were rebuilt in less than a decade. Uniformity of style and structure was the predictable result. The Italianate commercial row building proved to be remarkably adaptable, and worked equally well for bank, office, sales, storage or light manufacture. The form had made its appearance in northern cities in the 1850s, but in Richmond at that time commercial activity was most often pursued on the ground floor of a three-story pitched-roof dwelling. After the war, the new loft buildings were exclusively commercial, generally three or four stories tall, brick, and flat-roofed. Though they kept as their structural module the twenty- or twenty-five-foot width of the lot, a single design often unified the façade of several adjacent structures. In style, Main Street in Richmond was a close cousin to streets in far distant New York, St. Louis, Baltimore and Portland.

The iron industry which sparked Richmond's economic recovery was important also in her physical regeneration, supplying much of the material for the rebuilding of Main Street. The street façade from Ninth to Fifteenth streets was a virtual cast-iron showcase; entries and display windows were universally framed in cast iron and a number of structures had complete iron fronts. First developed in the 1850s, cast-iron architecture had been enthusiastically adopted by rapidly growing cities across the nation, but the technology proved especially suited to Richmond's urgent needs. It was readily available, and utilizing precast and partly pre-assembled iron elements, buildings were erected with speed, efficiency, economy and, of equal importance for the self-image of the regenerated city, in the same high-style garb flaunted by great cities across the nation.

The Richmond Architectural Iron Works, destroyed in the war, was reerected less than eight months later. The Asa Snyder & Company Architectural Iron Works, rebuilt in 1873, soon employed more than sixty workers and did a $100,000 annual volume. Its specialties were iron fronts, vault doors, elevators, railings, parapets, fences, skylights and cornices. The Phoenix Foundry, on Eighth Street, between Main and Franklin, produced many of these items, but also advertised a line of cast-iron balconies, verandas, columns, window caps, sills and sash, and awning frames. These and other factories rebuilt Main Street, the symbol of Richmond's recovery from the disastrous war and the expression of her commitment to a new era.

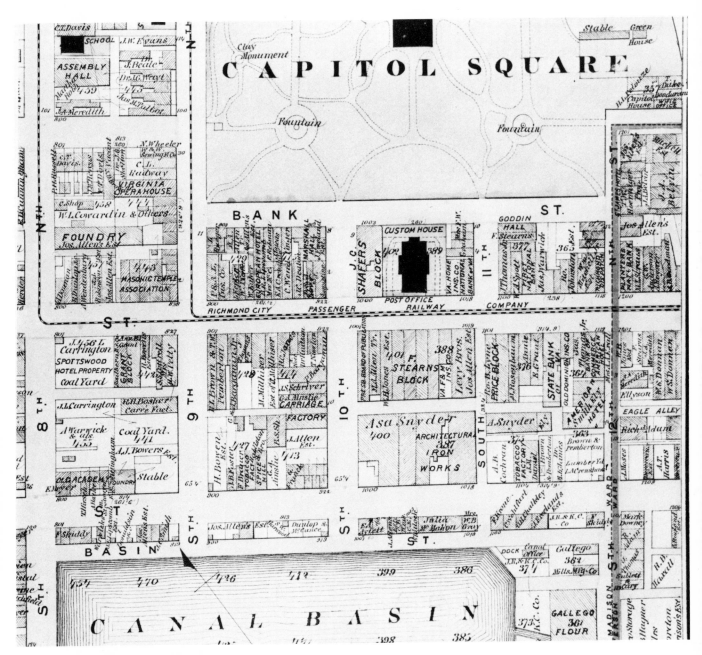

Plan of Richmond, Virginia, 1876
F. W. Beers Lithographic Maps
Columbia University Libraries

Main Street runs across the center of this photograph, marked by the tracks
of the Richmond City Passenger Railway Company. From Ninth Street east,
Main Street was almost completely rebuilt in the decade following the
evacuation fire.
Richmond was laid out in the 1730s as a venture of William Byrd II, and like
most Virginia towns of the period, was sited at the fall line of a river. Its plan,
a simple grid whose Main Street ran parallel to the James River, was enlarged
by Thomas Jefferson after Richmond became capital of Virginia in 1779.
The photographs of Richmond are from the collection
of the Valentine Museum.

Richmond, view north from Tenth Street, April 1865
Mathew Brady

Taken soon after Richmond fell, the view from the Canal Basin reveals the extent of the fire's devastation. In the foreground are the brick remains of iron foundries, flour mills and tobacco warehouses. On Main Street, the single surviving structure is the two-story granite custom house. On the hill above, unscathed by the fire, is the capitol building, built after Thomas Jefferson's 1785 designs.

Main Street, view west from Ninth Street, circa 1874

In the center of the photograph is about the point where the evacuation fire was halted. From here west, surviving brick houses preserve pre–Civil War scale and form, while in the foreground, the shape of the emerging city reveals itself— taller, the building line more regular, spaces between buildings closed.

Main Street, view west from Thirteenth Street, circa 1870

The architecture of the 1200 block—built almost at one time—has notable cohesion and stylistic uniformity. On the street level, slender cast-iron pilasters frame large plate-glass windows and support masonry walls above. An exception is the third building from the left, which has a complete cast-iron façade.

In the modern city of the 1860s, the individuality of separate structures yields to the total design of the street: buildings abut; façades are flush; windows are rhythmically spaced; heavy iron cornices, projecting forward of the façade, emphasize the flat roofs and uniform height.

This and the next two photos were taken by the Cook firm, which operated in Richmond during the last quarter of the nineteenth century.

99

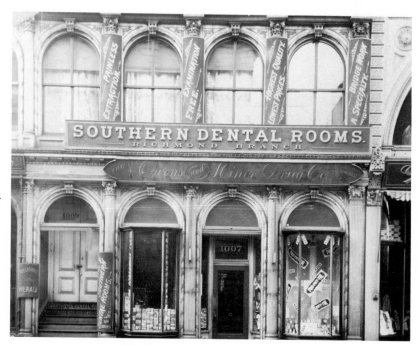

1009–1007 Main Street, circa 1880

This is the lower part of a splendid iron front which was the four-story façade of four adjacent structures, erected circa 1866. The ironwork was supplied by the Baltimore firm of Hayward, Bartlett. The façade is actually an enormous assemblage of individually cast elements. A single column, for example, might be formed thus: as many as a dozen square plates bolted together to form a base; several curved elements to form the shaft; and dozens of individual leafy elements to create a foliated capital. This method, a technical tour de force of the industrial age, was an economical and efficient way to achieve the richly decorative effect esteemed by romantic Victorians.

Lexington Hotel, southwest corner of Main and Eleventh streets

The popularity of cast iron continued well into the 1870s and 1880s; only small shifts in style marked the passage of time. The Lexington Hotel was built in 1873; its flattened arches are an updating of the round arches that were favored in the '60s. Cast-iron technology allowed iron to masquerade as the stone which inspired its design; here the iron pier at the building's corner mocks the masonry quoins on the upper stories.

100

HARTFORD, CONNECTICUT
Principles and Dividends

"Prosperity is our Duty," the liberal theologian Horace Bushnell preached to his Hartford parishioners in 1847; wealth is "one of the truest evidences of character and public virtue—a reward and honor which God delights to bestow upon an upright people." And surely, Hartford citizens were both hard-working and virtuous. In 1870, when Mark Twain joined the cozy literary colony which made Nook Farm, a hundred-acre Hartford retreat, its headquarters, the author could boast to his California readers that not only was Hartford the most beautiful and moral place that he had ever seen, but it had the highest per-capita income in the nation.

Hartford began in 1635 as a daughter of the Massachusetts Bay Colony and prospered as an agricultural market town in the fertile Connecticut River Valley, "the garden of New England." Main Street, on the ridge paralleling the Connecticut River, was formed from the "Road from Town to Wethersfield" and the "Road from the Palisado to Sentinel Hill," and formally named in September 1784. The city flourished briefly as a port. The waters of the Connecticut River also furnished power for milling and small industry. By the mid nineteenth century, utilizing steam power and rationalized production processes, Hartford achieved importance as an industrial center. In the 1850–1870 period, Hartford's population climbed from 18,000 to 37,700. More than half was employed by enormous new industrial establishments like the Cheney Silk Works and the Colt Firearm factories.

Hartford discovered that astute economic specialization also yielded staggering profits. Since its early days as a port, Hartford had been involved in insurance and banking, but after the Civil War years her rapid rise to national preeminence in those fields was indeed remarkable. The success story of the Connecticut Mutual Life Insurance Company, for example, was by no means unusual: its assets in 1861 were $3.7 million, a respectable figure for that time, but within a decade they had multiplied ten times over. Companies such as Hartford, Aetna and Phoenix held billions of dollars of risk in fire and life insurance. Hartford played a significant role in the settlement of the West; at one point she held more than $15 million in Iowa farm mortgages. Her money was no less crucial in making good the losses sustained through the great fires which periodically ravaged nineteenth-century American cities, and it was Hartford money that largely financed the rebuilding of Chicago after the disastrous fire of 1871. But it was equally true that Hartford money, in the last quarter of the nineteenth century, fashioned the dramatic transfiguration of Hartford herself.

With implosive force, the gentle, familiar silhouette of Hartford's Main Street was made to reflect the drastic changes in its economic structure. Vast corporate palazzos—an entirely new architectural form—overwhelmed the streetscape. Aggressively ignoring the conventions of nineteenth-century urban architecture, each one vied with its neighbor in scale, size, opulence and individuality. No longer did the building's façade act as a sheer wall for the street and a strong roof line define its height. These new granite and marble monuments were like giant sculptures whose deeply shadowed door and window openings and robust ornamentation were expressive of solid bulk and three-dimensionality. Cross and parallel streets in the vicinity of the historic State House Square were similarly impacted by new status-symbol construction. As centripetal forces pulled together the leading financial institutions, thickening the street and transforming it to a district, centrifugal forces pulled other users—dwellings, churches, parks, schools, small shops—to distant parts of the city.

Specialized and dynamic, Hartford was as committed to change in the 1870s as she would be once again in the 1900s.

The photographs are from *Hartford Illustrated*, in the collection of the Connecticut Historical Society. The book was published in 1892, but the views are selected to show the Hartford of the 1870s.

Geer's New Map of the City of Hartford, 1869
Columbia University Libraries

Long before this plan was drawn, most of Hartford's common, a space measuring some 500 by 600 feet, had been filled in by building lots. But the location of the Old Cemetery and the State House Square—both included within the original area—give an idea of its extent.

103

Main Street, view north from Sheldon Street

The view takes in the extent of the original
Puritan settlement, about a mile in length,
with Meeting House (later, State House)
Square at its center. More than two centuries later, the scale is still intimate, past
linked to present by continuity of use and
structure.

The clapboard dwelling at the left, with a
spirited S-curve pediment over the door and
eaves low over second-story windows, is
typical Connecticut domestic architecture
of the first third of the eighteenth century.
Next to it, on the site of an earlier Baptist
meeting house, is the brownstone South
Baptist Church, completed in the Gothic
style in 1854. Two structures north of the
church typify commercial form in the first
half of the nineteenth century; three stories
high, eaves to the street. The pedimented
gable of the more northerly structure reveals
its origin in the Greek Revival period. The
multistage tower in the center distance be-
longs to the Congregational Church. As
Main Street veers to the west, the pyramidal
tower of the Cheney Building closes the
vista.

104

Old State House, Meeting House Square

The State House, designed by the Boston architect Charles Bulfinch, is expressive of the grace and restraint of the Federal style. It was built in 1796 on the historic central square, the site of Hartford's first meeting house, burying ground and public buildings.

Center Congregational Church, corner of Main and Gold streets

This church is a descendant of the First Church of Hartford, whose pastor was the Reverend Thomas Hooker, the colony's founder. The high-style structure, built in 1807, was a far cry from the simple meeting house where the first congregation worshiped. Though it is almost domestic in scale, like the structures on either side, its columned portico and elaborate five-stage tower embellished with colonnettes, carved cornices, balustrades and urns proclaim the special significance of the church and the growing prosperity of the city.

105

Hartford Times *Building*

The 1850s marked an abrupt transition on
Main Street as the dwelling/store or dwell-
ing/workshop, like the one at the left of the
photograph, gave way to the large commercial block which excluded domestic use but
encompassed retail activity, offices and light
industry.

Aetna and Charter Oak insurance buildings

Almost directly across Main Street from the
Center Congregational Church, these buildings complete the transition from the gentle
romanticism of the first half of the nineteenth century to the bravura optimism of the
post–Civil War era.
At the far right is the sober Gothic Revival
Atheneum designed by architect Ithiel Town
and completed for art patron Daniel Wads-
worth in 1842. The Aetna offices at the left
display the dignified eclecticism of the
Italianate palazzo mode of the 1850s and
early 1860s. On the Charter Oak building
in the center, completed in 1869, the rich
detailing and piling on of elements express
the vaulting ambition of the Gilded Age.

Main Street, view north from Pearl Street

Grandly scaled and lavishly ornamented, the offices of the Connecticut Mutual Life Insurance Company, seen here at the left, echo the opulence of the palazzi of the merchant princes of Renaissance Italy. Of gleaming Westerly granite, rising five stories and crowned by twin towers, the building was completed in 1870.

Cheney Building

The unabashed power of the granite and sandstone Cheney Building—implicit in its active massing, taut arches and rough-hewn masonry—made it a restive, though brilliant, addition to the streetscape. Completed by 1877, the Cheney Building was a splendid example of the work of architect Henry Hobson Richardson and of the rugged individualism of the new capitalism.

JUNCTION CITY, KANSAS
Mid-American Main Street

Junction City, laid out by a partnership of three Ohio immigrants in 1858, was known as the "west edge of civilization" until 1866, when the Union Pacific tracks reached town. In the few years following, its population climbed to more than three thousand. The farmlands had been occupied, the town lots purchased; the land office moved farther west. The second phase of Junction City's development, the period from the 1880s to the World War era, was a time of filling in, gradually improving, making secure the mushroom growth of its youth.

Although Junction City first developed as a trading town for nearby Fort Riley, and served briefly as a secondary cow town, its continued prosperity was based on its position as seat of Geary County, as supplier to Fort Riley, and as a stock-raising and wheat-growing center. Washington Street, Junction City's main street, was the mecca for a wide outlying area. The hard-working farmers who came there to shop were Germans mostly, but also a mix of Easterners, Englishmen, Scots, Irish and Scandinavians. Here they were able to satisfy needs, if not a taste for luxury. Banks, groceries, livery and feed stores, agricultural-implement and hardware stores, mill agents, coal and lumber dealers lined the street. Their sober storefronts, usually built on single lots no more than 24 or 28 feet wide, were clustered on the few blocks north and south of the city park. Churches and civic buildings were to be found on Jefferson Street, one block east, or on the nearby cross streets. Built of the distinctive locally quarried limestone, these appeared austerely grand next to the small frame dwellings that filled in the grid. Five minutes' walk in any direction led into the countryside, the rolling river valley bordering the Republican and Smoky Hill rivers; and, west, to the Kansas wheat belt.

In 1900, the impressively scaled but conservatively styled new courthouse was dedicated. Junction City had more than 4,500 citizens. They boasted of the material progress that had come to the town in the fifty years since it had been the site of a Pawnee Indian camp: paved streets, sewers and water system, town hall, library and opera house. And, too, they pointed with pride at their location, scarcely ten miles from the geographic center of continental America.

The Junction City photographs were taken by the photographer Joseph J. Pennell during the years 1900–1921. They are part of the Kansas Collection, University of Kansas Libraries at Lawrence.

Plan of Junction City, Kansas, 1887
Sanborn Atlas, 1903
Kansas Collection, University of
Kansas Libraries

Junction City's plan reflects the orderly pragmatism of its founders. The grid was aligned with the orientation of the U.S. Survey; the railroad tracks were laid more than a decade later.
At the center of the grid was the city park, in the block between Fifth and Sixth streets. Flanking the park were ninety-foot-wide Washington and Jefferson streets. Other streets were only eighty feet in width.
Except on Washington and Jefferson, building lots fronted on the east–west numbered streets, with twenty-foot service alleys running behind them. But to reorient these alleys to serve the lots fronting on north–south Washington and Jefferson streets could wreak havoc with Junction City's orderly plan; this the town founders avoided by allowing the alleys to follow their normal pattern, though it meant that these passages would cut into the valuable frontage on the main thoroughfares.

Courthouse

The tall tower of the Geary County Courthouse emphatically marks off Junction City's site on a gentle rise between the lowlands bordering the Republican and Smoky Hill rivers. The courthouse was built in 1899 of the distinctive magnesium limestone quarried in the rugged bluffs that flank the river bottoms. The masterly use of this stone, so soft that it could be hand-sawn when newly quarried, is credited to the German and Swedish masons who were attracted to the area in the 1870s and 1880s by the extensive building campaigns at nearby Fort Riley. The optimism and enterprise of those who named Junction City in the 1850s were echoed a half century later by those who built the courthouse. "In old England, only cathedral towns are cities," wrote the journalist A. E. Richardson of eastern Kansas's early days, "in New England only incorporated towns; but in the ambitious west, anything is a city."

Firemen's Parade

The Fort Riley cavalry band announces the arrival of Junction City's fire brigade at Washington and Sixth streets. The tower of the Geary County Courthouse on Eighth Street can be seen in the background, rising over the two-story shopfronts on Washington Street. The façade of the Zee-Dee building, just nearing completion, is built of the same local limestone, while the 1880s buildings on either side are faced with brick and use limestone only as trim.

Bartell House

The successive additions to the Bartell House can be "read" quite clearly on its façade. The earlier sections are from the 1860s and 1870s, while the West Sixth Street addition is of darker brick, possibly the industrially produced pressed brick which was manufactured in Junction City after the late 1880s.

By 1910 the hotel had "commodious and handsomely equipped offices, large, well-lighted, and perfectly furnished dining room and elegant parlors" and one hundred guest rooms furnished with hot and cold running water, bath, telephone service and electric lights.

111

Washington Street, view south from Seventh Street

Replacing the old horse-drawn trolley, the electric interurban connected
Junction City with Fort Riley and Manhattan, some twenty miles away.
Electric lights illuminated Washington Street and the city park after the 1880s.
The electricity was at first donated by Cornelius Fogarty, whose gristmill was
powered by a generator on the site of the dam he had built on the Smoky
Hill River, at a point about a mile east of town.
Before 1901, Junction City had a municipally owned electric plant, though
the closing of the saloons that year resulted in such a severe revenue loss
that the town was forced to darken half its lights.
Junction City suffered two severe fires in the decade of the 1870s. Brick and
masonry replaced frame, and though ingeniously varied in details, Washington Street architecture acquired a generally uniform style.

Waters Hardware Store
Central National Bank

The conservatism of Junction City's building tradition can be seen in the
similarity of these two structures, though they were built more than a
generation apart.
On the hardware store, the end blocks on the cornice and the second-story
window lintels have "Eastlake" detailing, popular in the 1870s and early
1880s. Though its façade seems to be all of a period, the shopfront was
probably remodeled about the time the bank was built; note the resemblance
of the multipaned transom beneath the Waters Hardware Company sign to
the one on the store at the rear of the bank. The 1910 bank has an Ionic
portico that comes out of the early-twentieth-century Classic Revival, but
both buildings, in their squat proportions, materials and general spareness,
are remarkably kindred in spirit.

Washington Street, view north from Seventh Street, First National Bank at the left

By 1920, Junction City had accumulated a rich architectural heritage. Brick and masonry structures flanking Washington Street make up a lively fifty-year catalogue of style. Yet just a short distance farther on, the street thrusts past modest frame dwellings into the farmlands, with only the roadside trees to frame the vista.

Cleanliness, prosperity and order are written across Junction City's face: brick-paved street with no sign of litter; concrete curbs and sidewalks marked off by a wall of parked automobiles; electric lights on handsome cast-iron standards; a lively array of painted and illuminated signs.

Washington Street is an exemplary mid-American "Main Street."

STILLWATER, MINNESOTA
The Forest Depleted

Stillwater, Minnesota, then part of the Wisconsin Territory, was settled in 1843 at the head of navigation of the St. Croix River. At first, it was little more than the site of the single mill of the Stillwater Lumber Company, which processed timber from the heavily wooded valley to the north for shipment south to the burgeoning towns and cities along the Mississippi River system. Soon more than a dozen mills were operating along its riverfront, and when the village was plotted in 1848, there were already more than five hundred residents. The following year, the territory of Minnesota was formally established and the wilderness town was made seat of Washington County.

Stillwater had high hopes to become the queen city of the St. Croix, eclipsing even St. Paul and Minneapolis. While the dream seemed real, and the wood was the source of great wealth for Stillwater, the bounding pride of its successful German and Irish entrepreneurs was expressed on Main Street in brick and mortar. Frederick Steinacker opened his brickyard in 1859; by the end of the golden decade of the 1870s, when the length of Main Street from Nelson to Mulberry streets was almost completely rebuilt, his annual production was nearly a million bricks. Wooden shops on twenty-foot lots were demolished for the construction of massive commercial blocks on eighty- or ninety-foot-wide parcels. To the still heavily forested Minnesota wilderness, publications like A. J. Bicknell's *Village Builder* (1870) brought plans, elevations and specifications for the commercial designs current in New York, Chicago and St. Louis.

Main Street property was too expensive for any but commercial use. A new sixty-thousand-dollar courthouse was built on the bluff above its south end in 1867; its northern limits were marked by the huge Minnesota State Prison, built a few years earlier. Small manufactories were scattered on cross streets. Third Street, away from the hustle and bustle, was lined by a fine succession of churches and public build-

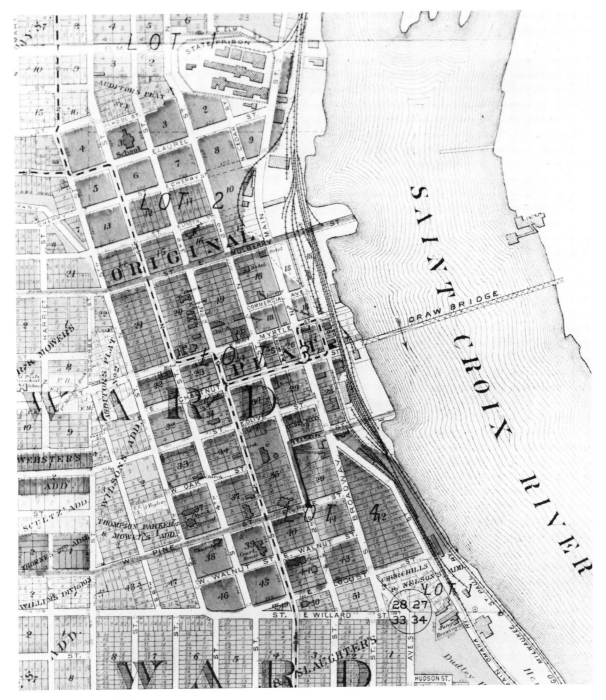

Plan of Stillwater, Minnesota, 1901
Washington County Atlas
Minnesota Historical Society

Stillwater's original grid was stamped on the site of the settlement that preceded it. It lay on level land along the St. Croix River and was aligned with its direction. Subsequent additions are labeled on the map with the names of the original owners. On the high bluffs above the old part of town, these newer sections conformed to the pattern of the U.S. Survey and were oriented to the cardinal points of the compass.

ings. Residential use was gathered on the high bluffs overlooking Main Street and the St. Croix River.

As the twentieth century opened, the pine forests had been depleted and the ax was still. Dairy farming and processing and the manufacture of farm tools replaced the sawmills, but profits were far smaller. The prison at Stillwater was replaced by a new one built a few miles south. In 1920, population was less than half of its sixteen thousand peak forty years earlier. For those who remained—and a 1920 survey found that nearly half its population had been resident for twenty years or more—Stillwater was comfortable, and well served by the solid masonry structures built during its lumbering years. Most workers earned their living in town, at the tool or shoe factory, at the creameries, and in the businesses and shops that sold to the neighboring farms. As the World War era ended, the motion picture had replaced the stage spectacular, but little else had changed on Main Street.

Now in the collection of the Minnesota Historical Society, the photographs were taken by John Runk, a commercial photographer whose studio was located above the Majestic Theater on Main Street. Runk's career spanned several decades, but the selection here is limited to the 1901–1915 period. They follow a sequence from the high bluff above the south end of Main Street, north toward the town limits.

View north from Main Street stairs

From the bluff above Stillwater's saucer-shaped business section—mostly
built in the heyday of its commercial lumbering prosperity—the view extends
from the Main Street stairs past the state prison grounds. Only scant traces
remain from frontier days. The small frame structure in the foreground,
gable end to the street, is one of them. On the brick wall of the empty lot
a few doors up the street, the pitched-roof "ghost" of another can be seen.
Behind Main Street, along the riverfront, mills and warehouses cluster along
the tracks of the St. Paul, Minneapolis and Omaha, and the Chicago, Milwaukee and St. Paul railways. The pyramidally roofed tower in the center of
the photograph is the 1887 Union Depot at Myrtle and Water streets. The
end of commercial Main Street is marked by the huge mill and massive
chimney of the Stillwater Manufacturing Company. On the distant hillside
spreads the massive state prison complex.

Main Street, from Nelson Alley north to Mulberry Street

Stillwater's Main Street is distinctive for its imposing array of similar commercial blocks chiefly constructed in the 1870s and early 1880s. In a few
cases, like the 1873–1874 Union Block at the left, which extends from
Nelson Alley to East Olive Street, the commercial block might occupy an
entire street front. More typically, a series of large blocks and smaller
structures alternated. At the street level, shopfronts vary little from the
thirty-foot norm, whether they are part of double, triple or quadruple blocks.
A strong cornice line emphasizes display windows and sets them off from
upper-story fenestration. Decorative surrounds add interest, but seldom
violate the essential flatness of the wall surface. To emphasize the roof
line, the cornice is a bold element, richly profiled and extending as much
as several feet past the wall. Brick is nearly ubiquitous, occasionally relieved
by the use of locally quarried limestone. Minor differences and similarities
engage in a seemingly endless dialectic.

Main Street at Nelson

At the foot of the Main Street stairs, Wolf's Brewery (whose cupola is seen
in the left foreground of the preceding page's photo) marks the southern end
of the commercial street. Constructed between 1872 and 1880, the utilitarian
brewery buildings display to good advantage the high level of masonry
craftsmanship practiced in Stillwater at that time. Note the carefully projecting stone coursing at the eaves and the handsome arched door openings at the street level.

120

Hersey & Staples block, southeast corner Main and Myrtle streets

Built in 1871, the Hersey & Staples block was typical for the diversity of its uses. There are three entrances on the eighty-four-foot Main Street front: one to a saloon (a corresponding entrance on the South Water Street side opens to its rear lunchroom); another to a stair hall leading to second-story offices and the Opera Hall above (note the taller windows at the third story); and one at the corner, giving access to the Lumbermen's National Bank. Two more entrances on Myrtle Street lead to offices at the rear of the bank, while yet another door opens to insurance offices at the corner of Myrtle and South Water. The imposing broken-arch pediment on the cornice of the main façade expresses the importance of Main over Myrtle Street.
The structure at the left, on Water Street, is the Union Depot.

Mosier Brothers block, northeast corner Main and Chestnut streets

This small block, built in 1888, conforms to its type in plan, while in style it employs the vigorous Romanesque mode of the 1880s. The corner entrance, boldly emphasized by the round projecting turret, is canted to gain maximum exposure on both Chestnut and Main streets with a minimum loss of usable interior space.

Joseph Wolf Co. block, southwest corner Main and Myrtle streets

Built in 1911, this block turned from nineteenth-century Romantic Revival style in favor of a spare classicism, emphasizing expression of structural system over decorative embellishments. Yet in scale, in choice of materials and in the use of such familiar conventions as the grouping of second-story windows and the decorative cornice, the design shows a healthy respect for local vernacular tradition.

View south from Commercial Avenue

Looking south past the Myrtle Street corner, where the interurban trolley makes its turn, back to Wolf's Brewery at the south end of Main Street, where this sequence of photographs began, one senses the structure of the Main Street environment. Here at Commercial Avenue, development is less even. The sophisticated commercial blocks on the west side of the street contrast to the plainer structures that house candy store and bicycle repair shop on the east side. Vacant lots and industrial structures signal the approaching end of commercial Main Street.

Stillwater Manufacturing Company, Main and Linden streets

The massive form of the lumber mill, visible all along the length of Main Street, looms large at its north end.
Millions of feet of timber were cut each winter, hauled to the river by horse or ox teams, and floated downstream to Stillwater. Here they were planed, cut, processed, and sent by rail to midwestern towns or by steamboat to the towns on the Mississippi River system. At the peak of lumbering activity, Stillwater mills employed thousands of men in town and in the northwoods lumber camps.

122

ORANGE, NEW JERSEY
Path to Progress

Orange became a suburb of nearby Newark, and of New York City, some twelve miles away, as early as 1838, with the construction of the Morris and Essex Railroad, one of the nation's first commuter lines. Yet for almost fifty years more, the community, first settled in 1678 by Puritans from the New-Ark colony, continued on its independent historical course. Most residents continued to earn their living in town, in industries such as hatmaking, whose history in Orange dated back to 1790, or in trade with nearby farmers. In the 1850s, Llewellyn Park, the nation's prototype romantic suburb, was laid out on Orange Mountain. And in the 1870s, suburbanization intensified when the Watchung branch of the Erie Railroad cut through the surrounding farmlands and opened them for development. Hills were leveled, ancient trees cut down, streams channeled, the fields cut into house lots. By 1900, Orange was home to more than 25,000 citizens. The placid village had yielded to a prosperous and sophisticated suburban satellite city.

Main Street began as a path to the "great Mountain Watchung," and even as the twentieth century opens, the sense of destination and movement along it is strong. As one travels westward from Newark, the mountain looms in the distance, and Main Street finally ends when it splits at the mountain's base. The path narrows around the small oblong of the Common and briefly splits in two in order to give street frontage to the house lots which were measured off its southern end in the eighteenth and early nineteenth centuries. Alternately widening and narrowing, subtly turning, Main Street's course reflects the natural contours of the landscape and the incremental process of parceling lots and drawing streets off its length.

The scale of Main Street is domestic, as it was two centuries before when the blacksmith, cooper and hatmaker set up shops in their dwellings. Dramatic contrasts in bulk and mass are provided by splendid edifices which reflect the new suburban prosperity: the flamboyant Masonic Temple; the richly detailed Music Hall; the ponderous Orange National Bank; the severely classical Strickler Library. Spaced at intervals along the pathway, they beat a weighty rhythm. The building line is irregular, spaces are varied, and cross streets intersect at oblique angles.

Through time, an unself-conscious process has zoned Main Street use. At its east and west ends, dwellings of "old-timers" and 1840s and 1850s suburbanites mingle with the few hotels remaining from Orange's days as a spa and summer resort. In the block or two north of Main Street are the town hall, the police station, the high school and the newspaper office. To the south, between Main Street and the parallel railroad tracks, service and manufacturing establishments include a planing mill, coal yards, livery stables and hat manufacturers. Commercial structures fill in the Main Street façade. These are of sober vernacular design, mostly built after the mid nineteenth century, when the community —having accepted, at last, the expense of a fire department— was spared from further disastrous fire loss.

The heart of Main Street is at its intersection with Day Street. Here are the banks and cigar stores, library and Music Hall, the trolley to Bloomfield. And here, on the site of the first Puritan meeting house, the tall brownstone spire of the First Presbyterian Church rises above them all.

The photographs, in the collection of the New Jersey Historical Society, are by Frank P. Jewett, a commercial photographer who lived in Orange and took more than seven thousand photographs of buildings and streets in this and neighboring towns from the early 1890s until 1917. They are arranged here to suggest the experience of moving from east to west along the Main Street pathway in the early part of the twentieth century.

Plan of Orange, New Jersey
Essex County Atlas, 1911
New York Public Library

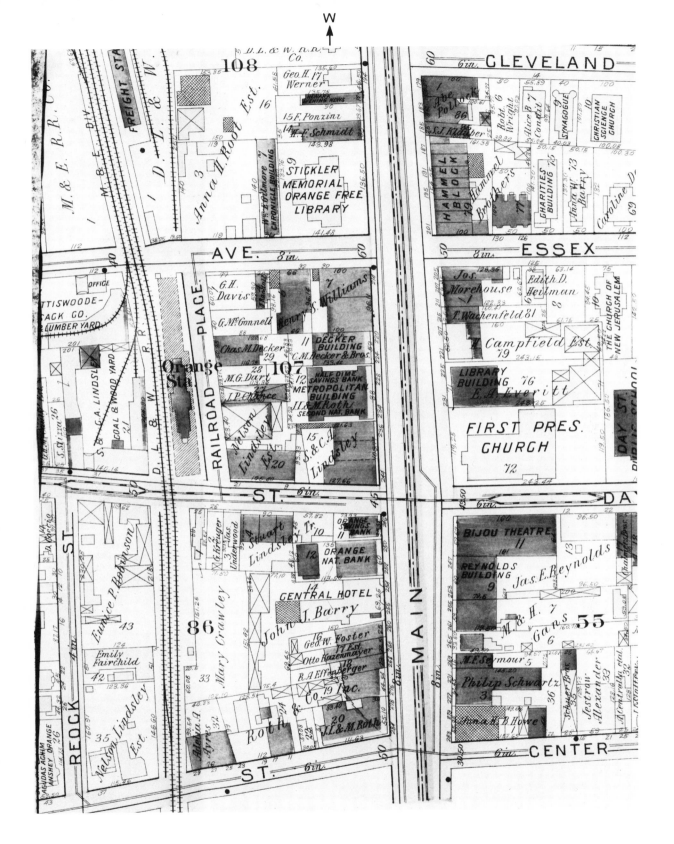

W

CLEVELAND 6 in.

108

D.L.&W. R.R. Co.

FREIGHT STA.

M.&E. R.R. CO.

D.L.&W. DIV

M.&E. DIV.

D.L.&W. R.R.

Geo. H. Werner 17

Jersey News 15 F. Ponzini

14 W. F. Schmidt

Wm. Zollmore 2 CHRONICLE BUILDING

Anna H. Root Est. 3

16

STICKLER MEMORIAL ORANGE FREE LIBRARY

Abe Pollock 86

S. J. Klucher

Robt. Wright 6

Alice B. Condit 7

SYNAGOGUE 9

CHRISTIAN SCIENCE CHURCH 10

HAMMEL BLOCK

Hammel Brothers

CHARITIES BUILDING 25

Anna W. Barry 73

Caroline D. 69

AVE. 8 in.

ESSEX

8 in.

OFFICE

TISWOODE-ACK CO. LUMBER YARD

S. & G.A. LINDSLEY

COAL & WOOD YARD 21

S. Mizza 26

Orange Sta.

RAILROAD PLACE.

D.L.&W. R.R.

G.H. Davis

G. McGonnell

Chas. M. Decker 29

M.G. Dart 28

J.P. Chance

Henry S. Williams

11 DECKER BUILDING

C.M. Decker & Bros

HALF DIME SAVINGS BANK 12 METROPOLITAN BUILDING

J.L. & M. Roth SECOND NAT. BANK

Nelson Lindsley Est. 20

15 S. & C.A. Lindsley

107

Jos. Morehouse 1

Z. Wachenfeld 81

Edith D. Heitman 8

Campfield Est. 79

LIBRARY BUILDING 76 E.A. Everitt

FIRST PRES. CHURCH 72

THE CHURCH OF NEW JERUSALEM

DAY ST.

ST. 6 in.

DA

6 in.

REOCK ST.

Alice P. Robinson 43

Emily Fairchild 42

35 Lindsley Est.

AGUDAS ACHIM ANSHEY ORANGE 43

Mary Crawley 33

86

Krieger 3

Stewart Lindsley Tr. 10

Thos. Underwood

Orange Springs Bank 11

Orange Nat. Bank 12

CENTRAL HOTEL

John J. Barry

Geo. W. Foster 16

Otto Rozenmayer 17 Est.

R.A. Effenberger 18

19 Jac. & Co.

20 J.L. & M. Roth

Alelia A. Ayres 32

Roth

ST. 6 in.

BIJOU THEATRE 11

REYNOLDS BUILDING 9

Jas. E. Reynolds

M. & H. 7

Gans 6

55

M.F. Seymour 5

Philip Schwartz 3

Anna H.B. Howe

Sluyter Bros. 35

Jestram Alexander 33

MAIN

CENTER 6 in.

View west from Oakwood Avenue past the Commons

To one entering Orange from neighboring East Orange, the length of Main Street—from the monument on the Common west to the Watchung Mountains in the distance—can be grasped in its entirety.

Originally several hundred acres in size, the Commons, first used for sheep grazing and later to rinse dye vats, was ultimately reduced to its present size by the sale of parcels for benefit of minister and church. As an expression of a quickening civic sense at the turn of the century, the Common had been beautified by new plantings, tree care, bandstand and water fountain, and embellished, in 1899, with the imposing memorial statue.

View from Day Street east toward the Commons

Commercial structures on Main Street's north side were mostly rebuilt after an 1860 fire. In scale they seem to defer to the grandly proportioned First Presbyterian Church, seen at the left with its tall spire cut out of the photograph. The brownstone church was built in 1812 in a conservative late Georgian style which found echoes in a dozen or more churches in neighboring New Jersey communities.

Breaking with the intimate scale of the street and symbolic of the shift in Orange's course of development were two stylish structures added in the affluent '80s: the Music Hall next to the church; the Masonic Temple farther east on Main Street.

Windsor Hotel, South Main Street, facing Commons

Orange's history as a resort began as early as 1804, when the Reverend Jedediah Chapman advertised for sale sixteen parsonage lots adjoining the Commons. He praised their countrified situation, and promised that they were ''well worth the attention of gentlemen wishing a summer retreat.'' The Windsor Hotel, built in the 1850s, was typical of the pre–Civil War country-hotel genre.

North side of Main Street

Immediately west of the Presbyterian Church, two structures side by side mark stages in the commercial development of Main Street. Number 217, the two-and-a-half-story frame structure, gives evidence of impromptu transformation from dwelling to shop, probably accomplished about 1860 by replacement of wooden elements with cast-iron shopfront and framing members. The Library Building was erected about the same time, but it brought to Orange a sophisticated and specialized form—the multifunctional commercial block—then gaining in popularity in thriving communities across the nation.

Music Hall (*Bijou Vaudeville*), *corner of Main and Day streets*

The Music Hall, built in 1880 in an eclectic Victorian Gothic style, was a flamboyant and ruggedly individualistic addition to Main Street. Breaking away from the constraints of street architecture, the brick structure was picturesque in silhouette, with a richly detailed façade. The social and recreational center was built at a cost of $51,000.

Orange National Bank Building, rear view

Concealed behind the sophisticated façade of the Orange National Bank,
and in Main Street's backyard, are storage sheds, liveries, artisans' shops
and other utilitarian structures. Note the false front on the pitched-roof
frame structure at the right.
The view is from the tracks of the Morris and Essex division of the Erie
and Lackawanna Railroad.

View east from Cleveland Street

An exotic crown to Main Street's nineteenth-century development was the Stickler Memorial Library, seen at the right. Built in 1900, the austerely handsome neo-Roman design was the work of the architectural firm of McKim, Mead and White.
Looking back along its length, Main Street is seen at its apogee.

Root home, corner of Main and Cleveland streets

A few steps past the heart of "downtown," an old homestead is a stubborn survival.

PENDLETON, OREGON
At the End of the Trail

In the remote reaches of the Inland Empire of eastern Oregon, only teams or pack trains could make the difficult land journey along the Snake and Columbia river systems through the rugged mountain chain that guarded the settled coastal area. Although Oregon became a territory in 1848, it .was almost fifteen years more before the wilderness along the Umatilla River was set aside as Umatilla County. Not until 1868 did the trickle of sheep-raisers and farmers make up a large enough number to justify the removal of the county seat to a new town on the site of M. E. Goodwin's 160-acre farm at a bend of the river in the eastern part of the county. Subsequent development was faithful to the American pattern, though telescoped into the brief thirty-year period that closed the nineteenth century.

The pioneer era was compressed into the decade of the 1870s. In these years, the last Indian uprising was put down, the town became a stage stop on the Utah-to-Walla Walla route, and Main Street was cleared of underbrush and cotton-wood trees. A brewery, saloons, gambling rooms, dance halls, hotels, livery stables and general stores were built near the first wooden courthouse. Wheat farming was taken up in the surrounding hills and sheepherding on the nearby prairie.

In the 1880s, the railroad freed Pendleton from her historic isolation. Completed in 1882, the Washington and Columbia River Railroad finally linked the frontier outpost with the Pacific coast. A neat town grid ordered formerly helter-skelter structures and oriented new construction to the double pair of tracks that passed through town. In 1884, six hundred and forty acres from the adjacent Umatilla Indian Reservation, confiscated by special order of Congress, were laid out for town lots and put up at auction. By the end of the decade, the town's population reached three thousand.

In short order, obsolescence overcame the pioneer environment. Permanent construction took the place of wooden shanties. The first brick building may have been built in

1880, although tradition also gives that credit to wool-trade pioneer "Uncle Jake" Frazier's 1881 department store. More than a dozen others followed in rapid succession. Among them were the *East Oregonian* newspaper building, the Pendleton Savings Bank, the First National Bank, the Pendleton Building Association Block, the Hotel Pendleton and the Golden Rule Hotel—community boosters and image-makers which joined in a lively competition to achieve the status and security of towns settled long before.

Pioneer pride in quick results went hand in hand with outpost provincialism. In 1889, a three-story brick courthouse costing sixty thousand dollars was built to replace the original wooden one. A new opera house went up nearby. Although solid, brick business blocks were stylistically retarded, interspersed with shedlike laundries, liveries and smithies, they made up a ragged streetscape. In the American tradition of town development, Main Street became part of a commercial "downtown," with residential use pushed to the hillsides north and south of town. Scarcely a half mile in length, Main Street extended only from the railroad depot to the river landing and was soon overwhelmed by the outward expansion of the town grid.

The 1893 financial crisis dealt a severe blow to the purchase power of wheat farmers and stock-raisers who traded on Main Street. Development slowed abruptly. Alongside braggadocio brick blocks, raw pioneer structures survived for yet a decade longer. When prosperity returned in the early 1900s, it was more firmly based on mechanized farming and industrialized wool-processing. Pendleton had moved into the main stream.

Most of the photographs were taken by Walter Scott Bowman between 1900—before Main Street was paved—and 1910. They are in the collection of the University of Oregon Library.

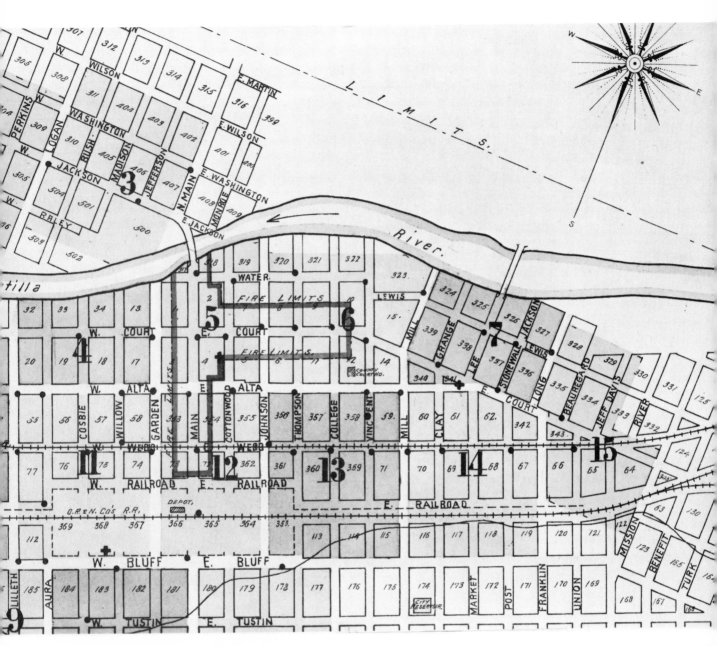

Plan of Pendleton, Oregon, 1903
Sanborn Insurance Maps (detail on p. 136)
Library of Congress

In the early phases of Pendleton's growth,
the town grid was oriented to the direction of
the Umatilla River and to the railroad tracks
that followed its course. Subsequent additions were aligned to the north–south orientation of the U.S. Survey. Main Street was
eighty feet wide, while cross and parallel
streets were usually no more than sixty feet.

135

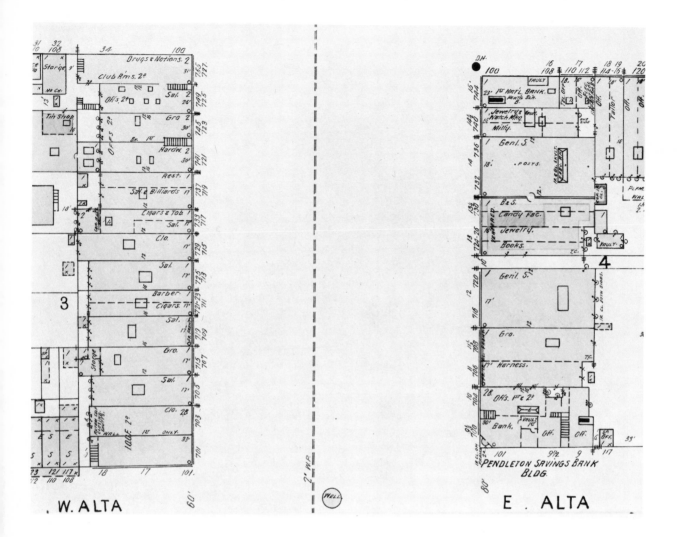

W. ALTA

E. ALTA

PENDLETON SAVINGS BANK
BLDG.

136

The Portland

In the pioneer community, the saloon filled the role of dwelling, restaurant, social center and public square. There were several dozen in Pendleton; the 1885 Mayor's Report indicated that more than one third of the town's revenues were collected for liquor licenses.

Main Street, view north

Pendleton's transition from remote trading station to budding eastern Oregon town was so rapidly accomplished that pioneer shanties often survived to confront sophisticated architectural forms. Scant years after the underbrush was first cleared from the level riverside town site, board sidewalks, graveled roadways and brick commercial structures had tamed the wilderness landscape.

Golden Rule Hotel

If by the late 1880s Pendleton's aspirations were those of a rising city, her architectural expressions remained faithful to the rugged frontier spirit of the past. A provincial grandeur, achieved through bold abstraction of decorative details, distinguished the Golden Rule Hotel, built in 1888 on Court Street.

Pendleton Savings Bank, corner of Main and Court streets

In backwater regions, vernacular design could bluntly defy restrictions of particular styles or periods. Built in 1890, the building of the Pendleton Savings Bank employed decorative motifs from each decade of the late Victorian era.

Main Street, view south

At the railroad tracks, which cross Main Street about where the trees are seen, the town comes to an abrupt end.

Horse-raising had been an important revenue source for Pendleton and the nation's change from horse-drawn to electrically powered streetcar at first had an adverse effect on Pendleton's economy. Later, pure-blood breeding developed as an important industry, and annual horse parades brought a flood of potential buyers.

This photograph was taken in 1907 by Major Lee Moorehouse, widely known as a photographer of Indian life and customs. He also served as government agent for the Umatilla Reservation and as mayor of Pendleton.

Main Street, view north (opposite)

Frontier chroniclers marveled at the rapidity with which the wilderness suc-
cumbed to civilization. Colonel William Parsons, Umatilla County historian,
described with glowing optimism a ride through Pendleton in 1902: ''We start
from the palatial and strictly up-to-date St. George Hotel. . . . We drive up
Main Street's broad avenue through a brave array of massive business
blocks, containing modern stores, wealthy banks, numerous shops, modern
hotels, and spacious apartment houses. . . .''

As population grew, the grid was stamped on the site of one-time sheep
pastures. On the distant hillside can be seen the ample dwellings of
Pendleton's early-twentieth-century prosperity.

140

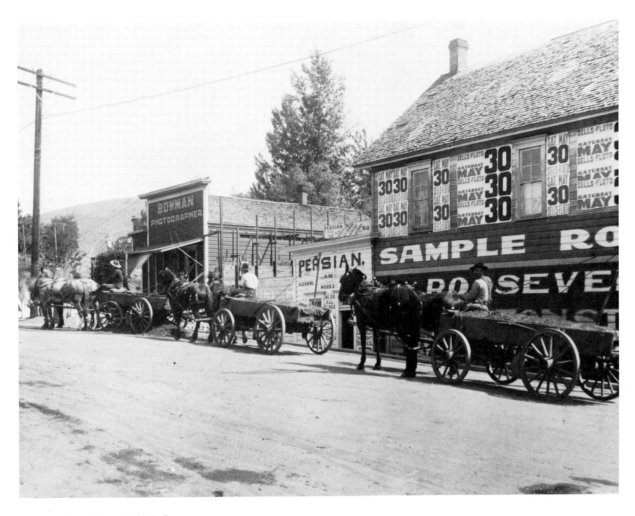

Bowman Photo Studio, Main Street

Walter Scott Bowman, son of a homesteader, was born in Pendleton in 1865.
A commercial photographer, he had his studio at the north end of Main
Street, on a levee along the Umatilla River.
Bowman was an ardent supporter of the Pendleton Round-Up, an annual
event after 1910 which perpetuated as a tourist attraction the spirit of
Pendleton's frontier past.

THREE
EXPERIENCE

7. Quality

American town-building was robust, pragmatic and democratic. New towns were built to be settled quickly, to function simply and effectively, and to hold out the promise of equal opportunity for all comers. Neither state, nor prince, nor church, nor foreign power determined urban form or quality; the control of the American environment was given to those who grasped it—generally promoters or speculators, who spent little more than was necessary to lure purchasers to Main Street. Politicians, with an observant eye on the voting booth, were the last to call for expensive civic improvements. If they were even aware of them at all, citizens saw the amenities of towns and cities elsewhere—grand avenues, landscaped plazas, floral decorations, public fountains, resting places—as belonging to princely traditions. Americans "will habitually prefer the useful to the beautiful," wrote Tocqueville, "and they will require that the beautiful should be useful." Here democracy ruled. The goal of creating a beautiful urban environment, one which expressed the spiritual and artistic power of the nation, seemed possible only as the nineteenth century drew to a close.

"The unobstructed tree-lined vista of the American street is America's chief contribution to city-making," wrote the civic expert Charles Zueblin in 1916. And in fact, through the nineteenth century, trees were almost the only embellishment of most towns. The practice of planting street trees, nearly as old as the earliest New England towns, was vigorously renewed in the 1850s as an aspect of the Romantic

Stockbridge, Massachusetts, circa 1880 (upper opposite)
Main Street
Culver Pictures

De Pere, Wisconsin, circa 1870–1880
(lower opposite)
Thomas Bowring; State Historical Society
of Wisconsin

Note the row of young trees along the board
sidewalk.

Las Vegas, New Mexico, circa 1890
Museum of New Mexico

With picket fence, grass lawn and shade trees, the old Spanish
plaza is dressed like a New England green.

Watertown, Wisconsin, circa 1890–1905
View down Main Street from Church Street
Henry Bergmann; State Historical Society of Wisconsin

The foundry-made watering trough was a common Main Street
embellishment.

Memphis, Tennessee, 1895
Court Square
Memphis Public Library and
Information Center

In 1876, fifty citizens contributed one thousand dollars each to pay for the thirty-foot-high statue, a centennial gift to their city.

Buffalo, New York, 1900
Main and Genesee streets
Detroit Photographic Company
Library of Congress

Buffalo's Soldiers' and Sailors' Monument was erected in 1884.

148

appreciation of nature and the beauty of well-shaded villages. The horticulturist Andrew Jackson Downing, whose writings were widely influential, proclaimed that street trees were the "outward mark of education, moral sentiment, love of home and refined civilization which makes the main difference between Massachusetts and Madagascar." Enthusiasts also hailed trees as "guardians of public health, which purified polluted air, cleansed pavements and, shading road surfaces, retarded noxious fermentation." Elms and oaks reached maturity slowly, but rapid results cou'd be achieved by fast-growing native pines, exotic ailanthus or poplars. The practice of tree-planting spread across the country; by the 1870s it was something of a national craze. Horticultural societies were formed by the dozen, Arbor Day was made a national observance, and hundreds of rows of centennial trees were planted along once-barren Main Streets.

Village improvement associations then looked past the roadside to the entire small-town environment. Enrichment of village life, it was hoped, would not only slow the flood of youth from agricultural towns to industrializing cities, but lure summer boarders and bolster sagging village economy. The sweeping by-laws of the Clinton Rural Improvement Association (founded in 1855, one of the first) were typical of those of dozens of similar groups formed in the post–Civil War decades:

"The object of this Association shall be to cultivate public spirit, quicken the social and intellectual life of the people, promote good fellowship, and secure better public health by better hygienic conditions in our homes and surroundings, improve our streets, roads, public grounds, side-walks, establish good grass borders in the streets and public squares, provide drinking troughs, break out paths through the snow, light the streets, remove nuisances, and in general to build up and beautify the whole town and thus enhance the value of its real estate and render Clinton a still more inviting place of residence."

In these years, the towns of New England, western New York and Ohio achieved their unique beauty. While fences around dwellings were taken down and the lawns between them made smooth and continuous, cemeteries, churchyards

Oakland, California, 1902
City Hall Square
Detroit Photographic Company
Library of Congress

City Hall Square amenities—clipped lawns,
flower beds, shaded benches and bandstand
—are evidence of Oakland's large scale
civic spirit at a time when the town was only
a modest-sized suburb of San Francisco.

and town squares were set off by cut-stone parapets, fancy wrought-iron fences or grandiose statues or fountains. A lacy bandstand embellished the town park and served as a focus for public ceremonies or pageants glorifying local history and heroes. The participation of schoolchildren, businessmen's associations, ladies' clubs, church societies and other community organizations was eagerly courted to repair, clean, improve and maintain Main Street.

In the 1880s, midwestern agricultural towns suffered serious population decline, much as New England towns had earlier. They, too, turned to village improvement associations, not only to enhance the quality of their environment, but to attract industry as well. Toward the end of the century, B. G. Northrop, the Connecticut reformer known as the "Father of the Village Improvement Society," praised the progress made by western states, finding that the cooperation and enterprise of their improvement societies surpassed that of the "staid" East. For the first time, a hastily built town might enjoy street trees, public fountains, watering troughs, plantings around railroad station and library, and rest facilities for farmers' wives shopping on Main Street. "If our social consciousness as a whole awakens slowly, it has its brief flare

150

of brilliance, too," wrote the midwestern novelist and spokesman for small-town living, Zona Gale.

The task of municipal improvement, largely begun as "women's work" in the 1860s and 1870s, became an impressive outlet for feminine talent as the century drew to a close. Women spearheaded civic consciousness from Hartford, Connecticut, to Fairfield, Iowa, and from Honesdale, Pennsylvania, to Pasadena, California. One female journalist, writing in the *Atlantic Monthly* in 1897, could boast that women's pent-up energy might even have force enough to "sweep this globe from pole to pole and neatly dust every continent."

The spirit of the Progressive era—and the sometimes hideous conditions of urban life around the turn of the century—called on the "obligations of city building." Professional

Cheyenne, Wyoming, 1908
Capitol Building
Wyoming State Archives and Historical Department

With the growth of government, appropriate public buildings were needed as much for their symbolism as for their functionalism.

St. Cloud, Minnesota, 1902
Post Office Construction
Public Buildings Service, National Archives

Upper Sandusky, Ohio, circa 1900
Library of Congress

Ossining, New York, circa 1910
Bank for Savings Building
William Terhune; published by Albertype
Company
State Historical Society of Wisconsin

The corner bank was often among the finest
of the City Beautiful monuments.

reformers rebuffed volunteer efforts, claiming that they satisfied the citizen with something less than he deserved. The
systemization and municipalization of civic services proceeded with missionary (and usually masculine) zeal. In
1889, the reformer Richard Ely lauded government as a
"God-given Agency" which could and should act on every
single aspect of urban life, from street-washing and garbage
removal to liquor control and poor relief. Professional
societies, periodicals, books and university programs in civic
studies proliferated. By 1916, Charles Zueblin could report
with pious pleasure that "civic health is attaining spiritual
proportions."

As we have seen, "Main Street" grew as vernacular expression. Neither a sense of history nor a sense of obligation
toward the future trammeled its youthful vigor. In 1850,
Andrew Jackson Downing could complain with only slight
exaggeration that "there had not, in the whole duration of the
republic, been a single word said, or a single plan formed,
calculated to embody past experience, or to assist in any way

Lake Forest, Illinois, 1930
Chicago Historical Society

Lake Forest was an 1860s gridiron railroad suburb, but a vision of the garden city was behind architect Howard Van Doren Shaw's 1913 remodeling of its main business street to include a landscaped square, arcaded shops and a quaint clock tower.

in the laying out of a village or town." In the haste and heady thrill of settling the vast continent, town-builders put immediately practical concerns above all others. And the thought that their society might owe a debt to posterity, observed the British historian Lord Bryce in 1888, "had not crossed their minds."

But as the century ended, a new tradition was in the making. In 1893, at the Chicago Exposition, an impressive team of designers, architects, landscape architects and engineers had combined talent and training to create a stunning urban ensemble that was without precedent in the American experience. Greeted as a "protest of the imagination against the ugliness of our cities," the achievement lent support to the subsequent City Beautiful movement. The speculator was forced to bow to the civic spirit; now a cadre of professionals considered the ways in which government and private enterprise could act to improve the urban environment. A boom in public-building construction seemed to promise swift realization of the City Beautiful. Architects, planners and civic leaders, cringing at the dark hues and picturesque asymmetry beloved by the Victorians, built public monument, city hall, post office and bank in gleaming white, and decked in classic garb to stand as glorious proof that the day of an American Renaissance had come. Clean and safe city streets, gracious open spaces, parks embellished with malls and statuary, handsome civic centers, provisions for public recreation, rational traffic systems, zoning—for the first time, these, too, became part of the American dream.

For towns and cities that had grown from no more than a broad and straight Main Street, a new vision was at hand. In *Main Street*'s Gopher Prairie, Carol Kennicott pored over magazines that pictured town-planning successes "like the town in California which had changed itself from the barren brick fronts and slatternly frame sheds of a Main Street to a way which led the eye down a vista of arcades and gardens." And she looked at Gopher Prairie, almost assured that she was "not quite mad in her belief that a small American town might be lovely."

8. Utility

While as late as 1875 Main Street was little more than a primitive roadway—dark at night, dusty in summer, muddy in spring, piled with snow in winter, and at all times littered with trash and refuse—by the end of the century it was drained, paved, swept, and lit as well as, if not better than, the grandest avenues of European cities.

Energetic experimentation in the last quarter of the nineteenth century yielded a wide variety of new materials and construction techniques for improving the efficiency of the urban environment. For Americans, the engineer was the "great artist of our epoch," and a remarkable characteristic of town, village or city, old or new, poor or rich, was its rapid and enthusiastic adoption—though at a staggering cost to the municipality and achieved only by voter approval of bond issues for each new improvement or the corrupting practice of letting out franchises—of the best and the latest that technology offered. In building the nation, mechanical progress was the evidence of civilization.

THE ROAD AND ITS CARE

The macadamized road, when developed in the mid eighteenth century, was hailed as a remarkable achievement. Formed by layers of tightly packed stones pounded into a nearly homogeneous surface during an initial period of "breaking in," it was an enormous improvement over the usual

Milwaukee, Wisconsin, circa 1905–1910
Robert Taylor; State Historical Society
of Wisconsin

The photograph shows the gravel bed of a
macadam street.

Ketchikan, Alaska, 1918
W. H. Case; Alaska Historical Library

Alaska's climate made wood-plank paving
practical long after its use had been dis-
continued in the continental United States.

rutted, rocky colonial road. But with more traffic, and larger
and heavier vehicles, the macadam road yielded a disturbing
accumulation of dust, and after a heavy rainfall the surface
was often transformed into a "broad slush-bed" with passage
across a hoary adventure. The Telford road, built up of firmly
wedged quarry stone beneath several layers of pebbles and
gravel, was an improvement, but both required periodic
sprinkling with water to bind the surface and control dust.

157

Des Moines, Iowa, 1907
F. J. Bandholtz; Library of Congress

Brick-paved sidewalks, concrete curbing and
metal drainage pipes precede the installation
of road surfacing.

Oil was later used for this purpose with such success that the
macadam road was popular well into the twentieth century,
when, covered with coal tar, it could even survive the punish-
ing treatment of the automobile.

In larger or more prosperous towns, cobblestone, brick or
granite "Belgian blocks" had often been used as paving
material, but for the emerging profession of sanitary engineer, such a road surface was an abomination. "The filth of
the streets gathers in ruts and joints, is recruited constantly
by new accessions of urine, horse-dung and silt, and diluted
by the rain, it ferments and forms a putrescent organic mire,
becoming in the course of time a noxious miasma," complained the *Popular Science Monthly* in March 1875. Although filth might be avoided by laying a concrete or brick
foundation, the hardness of such a surface resulted in an in-
credible din when passed over by horse or wagon. Wood-

Washington, D.C., 1907
Pennsylvania Avenue
Asphalt Institute

Asphalted in 1876, Pennsylvania Avenue was one of the nation's first streets
to be so paved.

Racine, Wisconsin, 1901
North Main Street
State Historical Society of Wisconsin

block pavement—smooth, dustless, quiet, and made relatively durable by treatment with oily creosotic preservatives—was a satisfactory alternative in some parts of the country.

Energetic experimentation in the 1870s developed and clearly demonstrated the practical advantages of bituminous asphalt and Portland concrete, used singly or in combination with other materials. Conglomerates also used coal tar, ashes, sawdust and gravel. Vitrified brick, laid with improved cement mortar, was an especially successful material in the Midwest. Engineering skills kept pace with improvements in surfacing materials. Pioneer efforts in the construction of sidewalks, road footings, drainage systems and grading techniques were undertaken by George E. Waring, Jr., a trained agronomist whose interest in street improvements dated back to his involvement with the Stockbridge, Massachusetts, Village Improvement Association in the 1850s. Waring was a forceful advocate of improved streets and argued for the advantages of a carefully drained, well-paved thirty-foot roadway over a sixty- or eighty-foot one that was rutted and muddy.

By the 1880s, technology could promise a Main Street that was easily and pleasantly traveled, but it was the task of succeeding decades to achieve it. While the well-paved and continuously flushed streets of the Mormons' Salt Lake City earned universal admiration, most travelers were chagrined by street conditions elsewhere. "The dust, waste-paper littered, was still deep in the streets," Mark Twain complained of New Orleans in *Life on the Mississippi*, and "the deep trough-like gutters along the curbstones were still half-full of reposeful water with a dusty surface." And the British journalist Charles Russell found that though the streets of Chicago, the midwestern metropolis, were "shockingly paved," none from New York to Niagara could claim to be better. Residents of Santa Ana, California, posted their protest at the corner of Fourth and Main: "The street is not passable, nor is it jackassable. All who must travel it must turn out and gravel it." And when concrete and asphalt paving was finally laid there in 1893, sidewalk superintendents gathered to gape at the "nine-days' wonder," thrilling at the clatter of horse hoofs over its two-block length. Continual

De Pere, Wisconsin, circa 1870–1880
Thomas Bowring; State Historical Society
of Wisconsin

This street corner illustrates the rapid
changeover in street-surfacing materials
that occurred in most towns in the last
quarter of the nineteenth century: from board
sidewalk and dirt roadway on the side street,
to machine-cut stone sidewalk paving blocks
and macadamized Main Street.

Hamburg, New York
John Van Epps; Library of Congress

The photograph records the ceremony initiating the paving of Main Street
with brick.

Hartford, Connecticut, 1885
Bicycle parade on Main Street
F. L. Hale; Library of Congress

Organizations like the League of American Wheelmen, formed in 1880, spearheaded the drive for improved roadways. Hartford's manufacturers pioneered in bicycle design and production.

digging up to lay new sewer or gas lines was destructive of street surfaces. Often deterioration was nearly complete before repair was undertaken.

Public demand for better roads was fomented by the bicycling craze of the 1880s, and then by the enthusiastic acceptance of the automobile in the early 1900s. Municipalities could no longer go it alone. In 1893, Congress voted a ten-thousand-dollar appropriation for a Roads Inquiry by the Department of Agriculture to disseminate information on better methods of road construction and maintenance. And in 1916, with the Federal Road Aid Act, Washington was committed to a federal-state partnership for the creation of a national highway network. The 1920s saw the development of modern road engineering; Main Street—banked, drained, widened, curbed and paved—was on the through route.

Street cleaning was a difficult problem even after farm animals were banned from Main Street, generally well after the Civil War years. Soiling by work animals was a persistent nuisance, and so was litter. The variety of devices to aid street cleaning included wheeled waste barrels, horse-driven sweepers and sprinklers, high-pressure flushing machines and automatic sweep and suction vehicles. But until the 1890s, when Colonel Waring made New York City a shining example of municipal cleanliness by his remarkable transformation of its sanitation service—street sweepers were garbed in neat white uniforms and operated with military efficiency—the morale of street cleaners was low. Reformers prodded citizens to consider cleanliness an individual responsibility. In Hartford, Connecticut, or Carmel, California, it was the socially elite members of civic improvement groups who placed discreet green rubbish baskets at street corners or lobbied to make littering an offense. In progressive communities across the nation, citizens of all classes participated in the growing number of town "Clean-Up" days. By the early twentieth century, Main Street could boast a remarkable standard of cleanliness and convenience.

TRAFFIC

Wheeled vehicles converged on Main Street in ever greater numbers through the nineteenth century—wagons, carriages, chaises, buggies, coaches and carts of every description. Systemization of transportation began only in the 1870s,

Yuma, Colorado, circa 1910
Collection of Carole Rifkind

The automobile achieved popular acceptance in the 1900–1910 period through the publicity given to cross-country automobile endurance tests. This, in turn, fomented demand for better road design and surfacing.

163

Anderson, South Carolina
Good Roads Tour
Library of Congress

By 1910, the automobile was beginning to dominate American culture; in that year, there were nearly half a million motor vehicles registered.

Washington, Georgia, circa 1910
Library of Congress

Chanute, Kansas
Miller's Views
Library of Congress   •

To some observers, it might seem that the horse-pulled street sprinkler was
more effective in soiling the street than in cleaning it.

Shawnee, Oklahoma, 1907
Western History Collections, University of
Oklahoma Library

At the corner of Main and Bell streets,
street-railway construction, curbing and
draining went on at the same time.

when the horse-drawn streetcar, running on tracks embedded in the road surface, became commonplace. In one town after another, streetcar transportation stretched Main Street into the suburbs and encouraged more intensive use of "downtown" for shoppers crowding in from outlying areas. Even in small towns, regularly scheduled streetcar service extended business into the evening hours and—for the first time—brought individual family members to Main Street.

Electrified streetcars—first successfully used on a wide scale in 1888—set the pattern for urban transportation for the next generation. Electric streetcars went farther and faster than the horse-drawn ones and made Main Street part of an intricate interurban network. In larger towns, streetcar lines followed the town grid, and transfers between cars allowed passengers to travel to distant parts of town. So intricate was the electric-trolley network that—with several dozen transfers—it was possible to travel from New York to Boston, and almost to Chicago.

Streetcar companies were often required to contribute

Topeka, Kansas, circa 1900
Library of Congress

Jacksonville, Florida, 1910
Main Street palms
Irving Underhill; Library of Congress

167

Kankakee, Illinois, circa 1915
Albertype Company; Library of Congress

toward the cost of street paving and cleaning. For the first time, snow removal was regularly undertaken, to allow trolleys free passage—although this created problems for horse-drawn vehicles, which had generally been pulled on runners over winter snow.

The electric streetcar seemed to be the perfect Main Street conveyance. Cheap, fast, safe, convenient and well-adapted to the grid, it carried as many as fourteen billion passengers a year. But by the World War era, the automobile was already providing formidable competition.

The varying speeds of auto and trolley caused serious traffic congestion—often excruciating at intersections—and endangered the safety of alighting passengers and moving pedestrians. Early controls limited automobiles to the right side of the road, their speed limit to eight or ten miles an hour, and forbade them to cut corners or park freely on Main Street. Progressively stricter limits controlled pedestrian traffic as well. "Jaywalking" was forbidden and so was crossing outside marked intersections or against traffic signals. Public sympathy favored vehicular transportation. Lord Bryce had noticed the tendency a generation earlier. "In America," he wrote, "no one walks if he can help it."

Hillsboro, Texas, circa 1920
Library of Congress

In this agricultural town, the horse-drawn wagon shared a comfortable truce
with the internal combustion engine.

TELEGRAPH, TELEPHONE, LIGHTING

"The Americans seem to be particularly attracted by motive powers," observed the keen Swedish traveler Frederica Bremer in the mid nineteenth century, "by any method of expediting movement and accelerating communication. Anything which can give life and action goes most speedily ahead." She particularly noted telegraph wires, strung along the path of railroad lines from state to state, city to city, from one Main Street to the next. Telephone wires came next. The first intercity line was put into use in 1879 and a telephone exchange was a standard asset of most fair-sized towns. When the original Bell Company patents expired in 1893, independent companies provided service to even the smallest community. Electricity supplied by a central generator also came into general use about this time. Telegraph, telephone and electric wires—as many as a hundred lines supported on a single row of poles—spread a thick canopy over Main Street.

Americans were slow to react to the ugliness of utility wires. While European cities had since the 1870s been carrying out ambitious plans to install utility wires underground, not until the 1880s did New York City become the first American municipality to respond to the unsightliness and potential dangers of above-ground wires and require utility companies to rent municipally owned underground conduits. In the West, Los Angeles—whose air space had been blanketed by a forest of wires from seven competing utility companies—pioneered in the move to put wires underground. The early-twentieth-century groundswell of civic improvement saw the policy adopted in a number of cities and towns. But this was by no means the rule. In the American tradition of town-building, businessmen remained firm in their conviction that the interests of wise municipal management were better served by economy than by amenity.

Each decade offered new improvements in the progress of illuminating Main Street—enthusiastically accepted, but abandoned when obsolete. Though kerosene was still in use for street lighting as late as the 1860s, most municipalities had already installed gas mains on the main streets, some-

Black River Falls, Wisconsin, circa 1890
C. J. Van Schaick; State Historical Society of Wisconsin

The installation of telephone poles was a mark of progress for turn-of-the-century citizens. Only the next generation, who accepted convenient communication as a matter of course, deplored their ugliness.

Salt Lake City, Utah, 1908
West side of Main Street

C. R. Savage; Utah State Historical
Society

times securing free light in exchange for granting the service franchise. After the late 1870s, the brilliant glare of the wire-suspended electric arc light was added to illuminate street intersections. And with the development and prompt utilization of Edison's incandescent lamp—it was patented in 1880 and by 1888 there were almost six hundred central power stations in operation—electricity seemed bound to rapidly replace gas on Main Street. Even the *American Gas Light Journal,* in 1889, hailed electric lighting as a guardian against fire, a contributor to the diffusion of knowledge and an "enemy of the thief." But in shopwindow or at curbside, incandescent gas lighting, vastly improved through the use of a gas mantle, continued to compete with electric lighting almost until the First World War era. Improvements of both types dramatically increased the level of street illumination.

As important as the practical advantages of electricity was its symbolic significance in confirming the material success of a new town, or the aspirations of a poor one. "At Guthrie I saw the sparkling globes throw their brilliant light on plank barracks, built a year before," wrote the French traveler DeRousiers. And at night on the bleak Kansas plains, the distant town was a "garden of lights," said William Allen White in the *Atlantic Monthly*. "At such a time, one does not recall the geometrically exact angles of the streets and the grey dust upon the unpainted houses."

Scranton, Pennsylvania, 1911
Horgan; Library of Congress

The Courthouse Square, lit by gaslight, was photographed at 10 p.m.

9. Activity

The sound of Carol Kennicott's footsteps echoed through ten thousand towns from Albany to San Diego when the heroine of Sinclair Lewis's *Main Street* made her thirty-two-minute walk through Gopher Prairie. She heard only the soft tones of a gossiping couple outside Dyer's Drug Store, the squeak of a lumber wagon, the rattle of a Ford, the whine of the peanut roaster in the Greek candy store—and silence. She saw only an "unsparing, unapologetic ugliness."

For post–World War I idealists—who had visions of a towered city by-passed by sweeping highways or a clean garden city with quaint architecture and curving lanes—the straight and wide Main Street that was at the heart of the American urban tradition was anathema. And the quality of the social experience was, if anything, even worse. "If they can't build shrines, out here on the prairie," raged Carol, observing the shopfront loafers, "surely there's nothing to prevent their buying safety razors!"

But through most of their history, and especially in the optimistic decades of the first third of the twentieth century, Americans regarded Main Street with pride. There it was—and it worked well for the simple requirements of daily living. In the process of settling a nation, making a living and getting ahead, few expected anything more. Lewis's grim caricature of the Main Street experience deserves to be placed next to the recollections of other American novelists, for whom Main Street was part of a cherished past, and whose memories fondly grasped impression of activity, move-

Kingfield, Maine, circa 1900
Chansonnetta Emmons; Culver Pictures

Bisbee, Arizona, circa 1906-1907
Brewery Gulch
Gemm; Arizona Historical Society Library

ment, form, texture and color, and tightly wove them into the homely fabric of youth, maturity and old age.

Noises were vivid in memory. Clatter, whistles, gongs, horns, shouts, calls, street songs in many languages resounded through burgeoning industrial, commercial and transportation centers. Ox wagons, mule teams and bull carts added rustic noises to towns in the developing South. "Omph! dis-yeh town is busy. . . . Looks like jes' evybody is a-makin' money," exclaims a citizen of the town of Suez, county of Clearwater, state of Dixie in a novel by southerner George W. Cable.

Evening sounds, before the early autos left their bellowing trail of turbulence, were soft, even in rapidly growing west-

Midland, Pennsylvania,
January 1941
Jack Delano; Library of Congress

East Moline, Illinois
Library of Congress

ern cities: ". . . the firefly lights of silent bicycles gliding by in pairs or trios . . . surreys rumbled lightly by with the plod-plod of honest old horses . . . the glitter of whizzing sparks from a runabout or buggy . . . the sharp decisive footbeats of a trotter . . ." wrote Booth Tarkington. Quiet, too, were southern villages that defied growth, slowly failing midwestern agricultural towns, and old towns "touched with the hue of decay" along New England's shores or in its remote hills, enlivened only in summer by the gay noises of city boarders. What do people do in such towns during the long winter? "Do?" replies an old-timer in Dorothy Canfield Fisher's novel about old New England, "Why we jes' live."

On the frontier, men moved through noisily and quickly, though mining town, cattle town, oil town, lumbering town— each had a rhythm of its own. In *Roughing It*, Mark Twain remembered the movement and noise of Virginia City with "its military companies, fire companies, brass bands, wide-open gambling palaces, political pow-wows, civic processions, street-fights, murders, inquests, riots." And Edna Ferber recalled the furious scramble of a later oil town in Oklahoma: "Fields oozed slimy black; oil rigs clanked; false-front wooden shacks lined a one-street village. Dance halls. Brothels. Gunmen. Heat. Flies. Dirt. Crime. The clank of machinery. The road of traffic boiling over a road never meant for more than a plodding wagon."

179

By day, maneuvering through sidewalks of prosperous towns might be a crowded and nerve-racking experience, but by night, the pedestrian could join in a tranquil window-watching parade of prim matrons and proper gentlemen who marched to the tune of the hurdy-gurdy man. In graceful old towns painted a sooty gray by huge smoking factories, natives met immigrant workers on Main Street with gloom and suspicion. Large construction projects—the railroad, waterworks or street-paving—brought Irish, Chinese, Negroes or Italians to Main Street. "But forward with American progress. Italian workmen came in gangs to our town, brought there by a contractor. A strange language was heard up and down our streets. Now, a seemingly vast enterprise to us, the sewer and the new brick pavement were being laid all the way from the head of Main Street," Sherwood Anderson's *Memoirs* recalled.

In some towns, memories of social changes were gentler. Petersburg, Illinois, had "two railroads, several coal mines, a woolen mill, several grist mills, some factories, a small

Somerset, Pennsylvania, circa 1910
Chautauqua Week
Library of Congress

Summersville, West Virginia, September 1942
John Collier; Library of Congress

Watertown, Wisconsin, circa 1905
Henry Bergmann; State Historical Society
of Wisconsin

Somerset, Ohio, Summer 1938
Ben Shahn; Library of Congress

181

Medford, Oregon, August 1939
Main drugstore corner in town
Dorothea Lange; Library of Congress

brewery and a winery," Edgar Lee Masters recalled of his boyhood town. "People had come there from Maryland, Virginia, Kentucky, Tennessee, New Jersey. And the Germans in town and about gave a liberal character to the inhabitants. The Americans were a lively people, full of the joy of living and of a great hospitality."

The village green or the town square was a center of social life. Vachel Lindsay remembers a town in Fulton County: "Every evening the courthouse square is pretty well crowded with men, women, and children with no other attraction than to meet a sober, orderly, well dressed and handsome company. The hotter the evenings, the bigger the crowd, because it is pleasanter in the breezy square than even in pleasant homes." Old men sat on shaded benches, farmers sold their wares, housewives gossiped, small boys played quoits, little girls roller-skated. "With an accompanying whir of roller-bearings and crash of steel on concrete, we swept round and round the square or puffed up the slight incline to the Main Street steps and swooped down again with a last-minute right-angled swing to avoid a ducking in the fountain," Helen Santmyer, an Ohioan, writes of her youth.

The hitching post around the courthouse square was a kind of public calendar for the days, weeks and seasons. "On court days and elections, I remember, they quite filled the rack and overflowed to the posts in front of the courthouse, which stood on its own ground a little off from the square," wrote Mary Austin. At election time, crowds gathered to hear the speeches. When court was in session, lawyers and loafers milled around in the open space, waiting for news from within.

Politics spread to the train depot, post office and general store. Harriet Beecher Stowe speaks of the leisurely moments that townsmen spent "discussing politics or theology from the top of the codfish or mackerel barrels while their wives and daughters were shopping among the dress goods and ribbons." Poet Vachel Lindsay's "Editorial to the Wise Man in the Metropolis Concerning the Humble Agricultural Village in

Telluride, California, September 1940
Former bank, now an Elks club
Russell Lee; Library of Congress

Barbourville, Kentucky, 1930
Knox County Courthouse
Caufield & Shook, Inc.; Library of Congress

Sheridan, Wyoming, August 1941
Marion Post Wolcott; Library of Congress

Central Illinois" promised him that "Chewing tobacco is still for sale, but rural free delivery had disbanded the central cuspidor club that used to tarnish yesterday's post office." In the South, prominent men in town continued to congregate at the post office to await the daily distribution of the morning mail. "There is the judge, three or four lawyers, the merchants, the bankers," editor Sherwood Anderson observed from the newspaper office in the alley back of Main Street. "This is a Virginia Town. These people have not moved about much. Not many new people have come in."

Social activity spread through the bank, the butcher and furniture shops, the grocery, clothing, hardware and millinery stores. With its striped awning outside and soda fountain within, "Mr. Galloway operated his drug store for pleasure, not profit," recalled Helen Santmyer, daughter of a small Ohio town. The corner of Third and Main "was the evening gathering place of my father's friends, where they told their best stories and settled the destinies of local Republican politicians. Daytimes, the store was mostly empty, except for children."

Saloons and liquor store corners were other favorite gathering places, though the Women's Crusade met with some success in banning liquor from Main Street. William Allen White boasted that the favorite corner in his town was occupied by a bookstore: "There the boys and young men of the town find a meeting place. There they make their appointments."

Sidewalks were the place for a few moments' rest, an exchange of views, a minute's gossip. The few old veterans or retired farmers who sat on store boxes or squatted on their heels along the curbstones by day were joined in the evening by youthful farm laborers and store clerks. They talked about books, Sherwood Anderson tells us in *Poor White,* and "tricks of their trades . . . new ways to cultivate corn . . . build a barn . . . religious beliefs . . . and the political destiny of the nation."

Shop, clubhouse, theater were powerful Main Street magnets. Glenway Wescott recalls the midwestern weekends of his youth: "As the sun hurried west . . . everywhere men and women and children were made eager by the thoughts of the night . . . for the night was Saturday night and they were going to town. . . . And in Middle America, in the numberless small towns that serve the people of the farms, there is no more magical time. It is the sweet reward of the long week's labor; it is their opera, drama, their trip to Zanzibar."

Vicksburg, Mississippi, March 1936
Walker Evans; Library of Congress

187

And if Main Street was the site of the small moments in an individual's life, it was—more dramatically—the locale of the great moments in the nation's history. Through Civil War struggle and the excitement of the centennial celebration a strengthened sense of nationality emerged. And corresponding to national fealty, there developed an identification with local place, a pride in specific locale, which was something new in the American consciousness.

Historical societies, pioneer clubs, patriotic and veterans' groups, fraternal orders and booster organizations—all participating in the periodic transformation of workaday Main Street to a ceremonial parade ground—were powerful agents in the enhancement of community self-image.

Appropriately, on Main Street—itself a distant relative of the straight and broad military avenues of the Renaissance—the first parades were military musters. Independence Day, observed in church ceremony since 1777, had moved to the street, where early practice favored morning burlesque parades of "Horribles," followed by sober afternoon displays of military pomp. Already by the 1850s the circus parade, a mile-long trail of glitter and gold, was another familiar Main Street sight.

Proliferating patriotic societies swelled parade ranks and new patriotic occasions expanded parade opportunity. Leading the procession in the 1870s were the veterans of the Grand Army of the Republic, whose huge encampments were preceded by lengthy parades which the whole town turned out to watch. The Sons of the American Revolution, the Society of the Army of the Potomac, the Society of the War of 1812, Veterans of the Mexican War, the Loyal Legion of Officers of the Union, Veterans of the Spanish-American War and the American Legion were among others to march on Main Street. Memorial Day, first celebrated in 1869, recognized Civil War veterans; the Labor Day parade in 1882 showed the spirit of the labor movement and the "great vital force of the Nation"; Patriots' Day was first observed on April 19, 1894; and the "cult of the flag," which had gathered force in the 1880s and 1890s, reached fulfillment in the early 1900s

Mayville, North Dakota, 1908
Fourth of July Parade
Library of Congress

Deadwood, South Dakota, July 4, 1882
Eleutherian Mills Historical Library

189

when Flag Day was widely observed as a day of reverence. William Allen White remembered a Kansas parade: "Eldorado silver cornet band in splendid regalia . . . volunteer fire department pulling the old pumping engine . . . the squadron of Mexican War veterans, all bearded . . . a half-dozen colonels and captains sashed and horsed and panoplied in military pomp."

In the early 1900s, the parade march expanded to a dramatic pageant, sometimes a vast outdoor theatrical in woodland park or distant field, but more often a procession of civic or patriotic floats drawn along Main Street. Breathing deeply of the Progressive Spirit, pageantry offered the opportunity to instruct, entertain, display love of country and accomplish worthwhile reform. The first of these splendid productions was put on in Massachusetts in 1909, when townspeople memorialized events from colonial history and thereby raised funds for the maintenance of town green and monument. Among hundreds of other communities that followed suit were Evansville, Illinois; Rock Hill, South Carolina; Ripon, Wisconsin; Reno, Nevada; and San Gabriel, California. Pageants were hailed as a way of unifying the community and arousing interest in its progress and future development. In the pre–World War era, the love of local place and the love of country were tightly entwined, and both were intense.

After the 1890s, parade ranks were swelled by the large numbers of "joiners" who became part of fraternal orders and social clubs—of the many, there were the Benevolent and Protective Order of Elks and the Ancient Arabic Order of Nobles of the Mystic Shrine, the Independent Order of Odd Fellows and the Prudent Patricians of Pompeii. Pageants and parades celebrated the dedication of town hall, library, high school, waterworks and electric light plant. Not forgotten were patriotic occasions, the birthdays of national or local heroes, and special regional, ethnic or religious events. Included in the lengthy calendar were Columbus Day, the Pendleton Round-Up, New Orleans's Mardi Gras, Denver's Mountain and Plain Festival, and Columbia, Tennessee's Mule Day.

Atchison, Kansas, circa 1912
Kansas State Historical Society

Ever alert to practical advantages, town boosters recognized the economic benefits of parades, and promoted town days—which brought shoppers to Main Street—in favor of the old-time county fairs. Smart businessmen, organized in commercial associations and chambers of commerce, capitalized on the search for regional and local identity. Parades and special events were held on Sauerkraut Day, Indian Day, Red Flannel Day, Apple Tuesday, and on a special day for virtually every state in the Union.

"What does a band mean to a town?" asks Sherwood Anderson. "Better to ask what is a town without a band?"

Presque Isle, Maine, 1940
Jack Delano; Library of Congress

Phelps, New York, Labor Day, 1907
Library of Congress

Boise, Idaho, circa 1910–1912
Steer in "101" Parade
Otto M. Jones; Library of Congress

195

Southington, Connecticut, 1943
Fenno Jacobs; Library of Congress

FOUR

CHANGE

10. Ghosts

The successes of nineteenth-century town-building promised to fulfill the American dream. In no time at all, it seemed, a peddler became a dry-goods prince, a land speculator a bank president. The golden continent was vast, and would support any number of towns; hamlets would grow to villages, towns expand to cities, cities explode to grand metropolises.

The youthful nation was free of memories, contemptuous of relics, indifferent to history. Here no law of primogeniture encouraged a son to preserve his father's land for his own son. Immigrants joyfully broke the bonds imposed by long association with one place and spread new towns thin across the continent, even without benefit of careful survey of topography, climate, resources or transportation—often with little more than optimism to sustain them.

So the unique story of American urbanization must be told in terms of its failures as well as its successes. Though thousands of towns grew and prospered, hundreds of others faltered and died—the inevitable result of too rapid progress, dispersed settlement, the "busts" that followed "booms," inadequate transportation, fierce competition among towns, climate, technological changes and exhaustion of natural resources.

The poignancy of the empty towns of the American West captured the popular imagination at once. Mark Twain's *Roughing It* enshrined the ghost town in literature: "All the appointments and appurtenances of a thriving and prosperous and promising young city—and now nothing is left of it but a lifeless, homeless solitude," Twain wrote of the western camp. "The men are gone, the houses have vanished, even the *name* of the place is forgotten. In no other land, in modern times, have towns so absolutely died and disappeared."

But western mining towns were not the only ones to become ghosts. One historian calculated that more than 2,200 towns, villages and post office stations were abandoned in Iowa alone in the century following the state's settlement in the 1830s. A Kansas historian estimated the number of ghost towns in his state at more than 2,500. The number of post offices across the nation has declined from 76,900 to less than 31,000 since 1901. Some may have been no more than the corner of the general store in a crossroads cluster, but others were at the heart of a small town, giving it a name, an entity, a reason for being. And the ghost town tradition continues to this day, not only in the small towns of the Ohio Valley, depleted Appalachian mining regions, deforested northern areas and the arid West, but in the very heart of the nation's largest cities, from the South Bronx to Watts.

In the nineteenth century a single blow was sufficient to transform a thriving community into a ghost town. One Kansas town, having lost a county seat battle to a neighbor, was completely emptied during the winter of 1888–1889. Departing residents of the former county seat gratefully accepted the offer of free lots in the new one, and actually carried their dwellings with them. Another, scheduled to death by drowning for a reservoir in New York City's water system, went the same route. Towns saddled with heavy debts sometimes solved their problems by committing corporate suicide; a Tennessee town, for example, sought to avoid its obligations by repealing its charter, and a heavily mortgaged young Kansas city bought an adjacent site, relocated its dwellings, and left its worries behind.

Americans were always prepared to discard an old site for a more promising one, so it comes as no surprise that they were pioneers in the use of portable structures; the mobile home and the space station are only the latest in a long tradition. In the early 1800s, New England Quakers, fleeing from British pirates, founded a protected port city one hundred miles up

Nevada City, California, 1852
Main Street
California State Library

There were more than eleven hundred self-governing mining districts in the western territories in the 1860s; only a few actually became incorporated municipalities. Fewer still survive today.

Keota, Colorado, 1939
Arthur Rothstein; Library of Congress

Continuous crop failure caused abandon-
ment of this Colorado town.

Katonah, New York, 1896
West Railroad Avenue
Collection of Katharine B. Kelly

Before their site was inundated as a reservoir in New York City's water supply system, the timber frames of Old Katonah dwellings were jacked up on greased logs and pulled by horse teams the short distance to New Katonah.

Ghosts in densely settled eastern states—unlike standing ghost towns in the vast spaces of the West—are more often buried by the sprawl of neighboring towns.

the Hudson, taking with them the knocked-down timbers of their former homes. During gold rush times, wood and iron structures from the East Coast made the long journey around Cape Horn to the California mining camps. Prefabricated wooden buildings traveled from north woods lumber camps to the treeless prairies. In America, "the houses are not fixtures," marveled the French journalist DeRousiers in the 1890s, as he observed structures being sent off in search of a city.

A trail of ghost towns followed the land booms that punctuated the westward movement. Town site speculation reached fever pitch in the old West in the 1810s, Illinois in the 1830s, Kansas in the 1850s, California and the Northwest in the 1880s and 1890s, and Florida in the 1920s. "When the collapse came it was like the crushing of an eggshell," wrote the journalist A. D. Richardson of the Kansas frenzy. "Again the genie waved his wand, and presto! the spangles and gold disappeared . . . cities died, inhabitants deserted, houses were torn down."

204

Maysville, Georgia, 1965
United States Department of Agriculture

Maysville's stillness is the result of the declining cotton industry.

Eureka, Colorado, 1940
Main Street
Russell Lee; Library of Congress

After the mines closed, the railroad spur to remote mining towns might continue only long enough to evacuate the last diehard. Nowadays, the four-wheel-drive jeep makes these stranded sites accessible again.

Tyrone, New Mexico, 1966
Bob Nugent; Museum of New Mexico

A company copper-mining town designed by architect Bertram Goodhue, Tyrone was a triumph of functional planning in a formal ensemble: depot, offices, a company store ("the Wanamaker's of the Desert"), school, hospital, library and housing were splendidly sited around a landscaped plaza. The drastic price decline of copper after World War I caused Tyrone to be closed down. Vandals attacked the marble-faced and tiled buildings; a highway was run through the plaza. The last of the structures was razed in 1967.

Concully, Washington, circa 1890
Washington State Historical Society

Concully's history is brief: a gold-mining camp in 1886; county seat two years later; a lumbering center while the timber lasted. By 1915, the town was a ghost.

Cimarron, New Mexico, circa 1905
Main Street
Museum of New Mexico

On the Santa Fe Trail, Cimarron flourished, with fifteen saloons, four hotels and a newspaper. But the town fell asleep when the trail traffic dwindled and it lost its position as seat of Colfax County. The St. Louis, Rocky Mountain and Pacific Railroad brought a wave of prosperity to Cimarron after 1905, but at a site across the river, leaving the old town little more than a ghost.

Mogollon, New Mexico
Main Street
Russell Lee; Library of Congress

In a ghost town, change slows almost to a halt. Though Mogollon's silver
and gold mines are nearly all closed, the bars still keep open on Main Street.

A change in regional economy, agricultural pattern or climate could empty a town just as surely as the collapse of a land boom, even if less dramatically. Georgia towns that flourished as tobacco inspection and storage stations were doomed when cotton replaced tobacco as the economic base of the region. Town-dwellers moved west to Alabama, and cotton grew over the discarded sites of town hall, warehouse, church, store and dwelling. Once-vigorous midwestern trading and milling towns had little to sustain them when the wheat fields were moved to the western plains. Even sturdy New England was victim. Westward migration sapped the strength of backwater villages and coastal towns, even though, by the 1880s, the summer people were moving in to fill the empty spaces. Villages dependent on cottage industries—dairying, tanning, cloth-dressing or barrel-making—could offer little resistance to expanding industrial neighbors.

Depleted mining sites are the most romantic ghost towns and, probably, the most numerous. In the arid West, plush hotels decorated with crystal and gilt, fancy opera houses, saloons, banks and supply stores grew overnight, and were abandoned as quickly when the lode ran out. A second epidemic of ghosts followed when the cancellation of government silver contracts sent the silver-mining industry into a long slump in the 1890s. Ebbing demand for specialty minerals—copper for electric wiring, or turquoise for jewelry, for example—also took its toll.

In thinly settled areas, the battle for a rail depot, a new industry or a county seat was often the battle for survival. At times one site had clear advantages; more often it was ambition, energy, business acumen and willingness to engage in cutthroat competition that favored one city over another. The town that lost its edge was a loser.

A place in a transportation network was undoubtedly the most critical factor in the success of a town. Through the nineteenth and into the twentieth century, virtually every generation experienced a transportation revolution; from stagecoach to steamboat, steam railroad, electric trolley and train, automobile, long-distance truck, airplane. Towns spawned by one transportation mode failed with the development of a new one.

Promontory, Utah, 1869
A. J. Russell; Oakland Museum History Department

This frame and canvas town witnessed one of the most thrilling events in American history—the Golden Spike Ceremony, celebrating the meeting of the rails of the Union Pacific and Central Pacific railroads. But within a decade the town was deserted. By-passed by a new line, Promontory contributed its rails as scrap metal in World War II.

Read's Landing, Minnesota, circa 1880
Minnesota Historical Society

The quiet of the Minnesota River is evidence of the decline of Read's Landing, a town whose life depended on the river trade. Before the steamboat yielded to the railroad, as many as three or four hundred boats spent icebound winters here, waiting until spring thaws released them to continue the journey to St. Paul.

Columbia, California, 1941
Herman Bryant; Society of
California Pioneers

Columbia's decline began after the depletion of placer gold in the 1860s. From a peak population estimated to be as large as 10,000, the town shrank to a few hundred, though it was never completely deserted. The Columbia State Historic Park was established in 1945.

211

Other cultures have buried their past beneath successive layers of civilization; in America dead towns litter the landscape like beer cans. Yet even as crumbling castles inspired the songs of medieval minstrels, the parched remains of western mining camps have inspired a vigorous American mythology. "The wickedest city in America!" proclaims the ghost-town tourist brochure. "America's newest and largest ghost town!" "The town too tough to die!" The lore of the western ghost mining towns glorifies violence, lusty materialism, the American tendency to keep moving, and optimism—the next place will be better.

Ghost-town hunting has become a popular pastime. Not only tales of bad-man exploits, but the compelling qualities of ghost-town architecture, draw thousands of tourists annually. Frederick Law Olmsted (the younger), surveying sites for the California State Park Commission in 1928, was among the first to recognize the historical significance of America's ghost-town heritage. He recommended the preservation of Columbia as one of the oldest and best preserved of the mother lode mining camps. Since then, the systematic preservation of ghost towns has become nearly as remarkable as the ghost-town phenomenon itself. From the ghost capital city, Williamsburg, Virginia, to the iron-manufacturing ghosts of New Jersey to the mining-camp ghosts of California, federal and state as well as public and private local agencies have taken an active role in the transformation of these relics into free-standing, open-air museums. While many restoration efforts have considerable integrity, others, intentionally or inadvertently, confuse the myth with reality. In "re-creating" ghost Main Streets, towns have been built that might have been, but, in fact, never were. An honest Disneyland may be more real than these surrealist dreams.

11. Growth

Twentieth-century America regarded change as inexorable and greeted growth as progress. Until the Great Depression, this faith was amply justified by the extraordinary expansion of her towns and cities and the gratifying prosperity of her citizens. "They were optimists," Booth Tarkington wrote of the Midland City leaders who worked for a bigger, better and more prosperous city, "optimists to the point of belligerence." The twentieth-century city expanded beyond all expectations, but in the wake of growth upward and outward, its center was left a dangerous vacuum. There was a price to pay.

In 1910, the U.S. Census recognized the changing character of American cities, including a new classification—the metropolis. Twenty-five metropolitan districts, containing nearly one third of the nation's population, were recognized. A decade later, there were at least a dozen new metropolitan districts, not only old cities in the Northeast (Hartford and Springfield), but new industrial cities in the Midwest (Akron and Youngstown) or the Southwest (Houston, Dallas and San Antonio in oil-rich Texas), and expanding trading centers in the far West (Salt Lake City and Seattle). With the automobile, the wide-circulation metropolitan news daily, radio, motion pictures, a faster-paced social life and the rise of white-collar occupations, long-independent small towns faced the harsh dilemma of stagnating or being swallowed by the spreading city. Now the city—not the farm or the town—dominated American life. Even Spoon River was metropolized.

Buffalo, New York, circa 1914
Shelton Square
Buffalo and Erie County Historical Society

A bold confrontation. At the right—representing the culmination of Victorian tradition—stands the weighty masonry mass of the Commonwealth Trust Company, the design of architect George Post. At the left, an early skyscraper masterpiece, is architect Louis Sullivan's Guaranty Building, a twelve-story, terra-cotta-sheathed steel cage soaring twelve stories from its wide-windowed base.

Lexington, Kentucky, 1919 (opposite)
Main Street
Kentucky Historical Society
Into space, the tall building projects the two-dimensional grid of the traditional city.

Salt Lake City, Utah, circa 1925
Main Street, view south from First Street
Shipler; Utah State Historical Society

The shape of Salt Lake City's Main Street
was a typical one for middle-sized cities in
the period between the two world wars, with
skyscrapers as tall as twenty stories rising
above the lower buildings of the nineteenth-century city. Note the tall building at
the left, actually L-shaped, though from the
street it appears to have the form of an
unbroken tower.

Seattle, Washington, 1916
Smith Building and City Hall Park
Asahel Curtis; Photography Collection,
Suzzallo Library, University of Washington

The Smith Building, completed in 1914, was
built so tall—forty-two stories were claimed
as its height to the top of its tower—that no
other Seattle building would equal it for
years to come. None did. A speculative
venture, the building was a New York type-
writer manufacturer's demonstration of
faith in the western city's future.

Dallas, Texas, 1942
Arthur Rothstein; Library of Congress

As Dallas's oil industry made her rich,
1920s and 1930s construction fashioned a
new silhouette of her skyline. Note the setbacks on the tall building on the left.

Miami Beach, Florida, 1925
Historical Association of Southern Florida

Miami's was undoubtedly the most spectacular of all the 1920s booms. Half sandbar, half landfill, Miami Beach was the site of more than 100 million dollars worth of construction in the peak year of the 1923–1926 boom.

Neither depression nor war stemmed metropolitan growth. By 1950, the census counted 147 metropolitan areas, inhabited by more than half the nation's population.

The tall building was the landmark of the modern metropolis. With the development of steel-skeleton construction methods and the high-speed electric elevator (both by the turn of the century), the traditional limits to a building's height (the space-consuming masonry walls needed for support at the lower stories and the distance that a pedestrian was willing to climb) were virtually eliminated. Not only the great cities of New York and Chicago, but small and middle-sized cities as well, achieved a distinctive skyline. In the first decades of the twentieth century, new office towers soared five, ten, twenty stories or more above the four- or five-story commercial blocks of the nineteenth-century city. Enshrining the corporate power of the East, or aggressively symbolizing the upstart ambitions of western cities, the skyscraper was

Hartford, Connecticut, circa 1935
Main Street
Connecticut Historical Society

An outsize echo of Hartford's old State House is the seventeen-story structure
that looms over it. Compare the Federal styling of the skyscraper—at the first
story and penthouse—with the early-nineteenth-century landmark that was
its inspiration.

Reno, Nevada, 1933
Standard Oil of California

Sincere attempts to create an architecture
for the Automobile Age—as in this modernistic example—were doomed to failure from
the start. In its very nature intolerant of traditional urban land-use patterns, the service
station threatens pedestrian space with
vehicular intrusion, disrupts the continuity
of the street façade and destroys the integrity
of street corners by replacing solid buildings
with vague indeterminate space.

Unidentified town, New Hampshire, 1944
U.S. Bureau of Public Roads,
photo 30-N-44-1855 in the National
Archives

The gas station exposes to public view a
seamy side of Main Street.

220

hailed as a national triumph, a glorious expression of the American spirit.

"Nearly 90% of all millionaires have become so through owning real estate," observed steel magnate Andrew Carnegie. The booming 1920s rewarded speculative land acquisition and building construction with extraordinary profits. Choice Main Street corners were cleared for new skyscrapers. Still other skyscrapers were clustered in new downtown locations—with little concern for the human congestion and disruption of the neighborhood. By the end of the decade, nearly five thousand tall buildings punctuated the urban Amercian landscape; thirty metropolises boasted at least twenty of the giants each. Commercial users—banks, offices, theaters, department stores, chain stores (by the early 1930s, there were more than five hundred retail Montgomery Ward, ten thousand Rexall, and fifteen thousand A&P stores) —thrived in the increasingly specialized downtown. Small manufacturers, "mom and pop" stores and marginally profitable services were gradually forced out of business or out of town.

Advertising—now an industry in itself—spurred the growth of Main Street. Made to order for aggressive advertising were the materials developed in the 1920s and 1930s: lightweight metals that spawned enormous futuristic signs on building roof and façade; neon and fluorescent lights that illuminated the nighttime city; shiny plastic and bright lacquer paint that dressed the staid Victorian city to the taste of the Jazz Age. With advertising came affluence—allowing the post-World-War-I generation to achieve "automobility." It seemed, for a time, that the car would contribute to the quality of urban life, ridding the street of the congestion, noise, disorder, and filth that resulted from work animals, allowing suburban development, and bringing customers to shops, readers to libraries and voters to city hall.

Main Street was furnished with wooden "policemen," traffic control boxes, electrically-timed stop–go signals (after 1924), mechanical parking meters (after 1935), and, in the effort to control auto speed, direction and destination, signs and signals of every conceivable size and shape, mounted on pillar, post and pedestal.

But, in large city or small town, the automobile's appetite for road space, parking space and service space was insatiable. The auto monopolized the curb, encroached on the site of the demolished town hall, and filled-in canal bed, and usurped the central square. Parking lot and service station bit into the town fabric, digesting corners, gouging holes in street fronts and devouring those intricate relationships that hold a city together.

By the early 1930s, with more than twenty-three million cars on the road, auto congestion, noise, vibration, gas fumes and traffic accidents were blamed for the degeneration of Main Street. And, two decades later, with more than forty million cars in use, the automobile's threat to destroy the city entirely seemed very real indeed. Behind the glossy Main Street façade, fundamental problems gnawed at the heart of the city. Pressing needs, for low-cost housing, health and welfare services, sanitation, transportation and recreation, as well as an obsolete political structure and an inadequate tax base were not to be denied for long. As the middle class fled from the margins of Main Street, it was replaced by poor southern migrants who were crowded into aging and deteriorating buildings. Around the central city festered decaying rings of slums and blight.

The automobile drew activity out of town, spread growth along commercial strips that thrust into the suburbs and blurred one place into the next. The year 1922 saw the opening of the nation's first shopping center; by the 1950s shopping centers dominated the retail trade—and impoverished the downtown merchant. The first cross-country highway was completed in 1927; by the 1950s, the federal government was committed to the largest public works project ever undertaken—a forty-one-thousand-mile interstate road network that freed the nation from the city. Main Street was losing its time-honored function as the place and the end of the road. The road went on—and on.

Macon, Georgia, 1936
Main Street
Walker Evans; Library of Congress

Though the parking problem was recognized as serious from the early days of the automobile, municipalities seemed helpless in the face of it. "Every day in big cities the parking problem grows more acute," the magazine *Automobile Age* reported as early as 1916. "We are facing something which was never foreseen in the planning of our towns, a thing which has come upon us so swiftly that there has been no time to grasp the immensity of the problem till we are almost overcome by it."

Pendleton, Oregon, 1947
Oregon Historical Society

Not the automobile per se, but its tremendous numbers, produced profound changes in patterns of urban living.

Richmond, Virginia, 1968
Richmond Newspapers, Inc.

Scaled to automobile driver rather than pedestrian, display signs and street lighting overwhelm Main Street.

Sacramento, California, 1965
Glen Fishback; Historic American Buildings Survey

Empty streets, empty sidewalks, empty shopfronts, aging buildings, poor people—litter left behind by a nation that moved to the suburbs.

Dunkirk, New York 1966
Milo V. Stewart

Paterson, New Jersey, 1970
George Tice

225

Akron, Ohio, 1965
Joan Sydlow; Photoworld, Inc.

San Francisco, California, 1976
Nancy Rifkind

12. Renewal

How did Main Street look at midcentury? "Much of what we saw was not pretty," recalls a midwestern mayor. "Slums, run-down business structures, poor streets and sidewalks, crime, disease, poor planning, exodus of business, you name it, we had it." But having survived a depression, won a great war, risen to world leadership, America seemed tired. Too tired to take up the challenge of the city, to deal with the complexities of town and city life. The middle class, whose access to the mortgaged home in suburbia was speeded by a massive new highway network, fled the moribund city.

Looking guilty-eyed at her troubled urban centers, America rejected her entire town-building tradition. There seemed to be only an occasional golden moment, in a Charleston, a Carmel or a Stockbridge. Mostly, America scorned her towns as obsolete, ugly, impractical, unfit. Aging vernacular structures were a drag on progress, not a link with the past. A patterned-brick Victorian shopfront was offensive, a taunt to the modern preference for clean lines and smooth surfaces. The grid was traffic-stalling, a remnant of the pedestrian city. For a nation whose goal was suburban, the economic, social and functional mix of the traditional city center was rejected, a relic of an obsolete life style.

"American cities were built mostly in spurts and grew in metastasis," pronounced the contemporary urban planner Charles Abrams, summing up the prevailing midcentury attitude. "While grace may show itself in an occasional 'money is no object' opus by Stanford White or a lesser genius, the general imprint has been that of the jackpot, not the temple." What was the cure for two centuries of history?

Mount Vernon, Ohio, 1949
U.S. Information Agency in the National Archives

Swift, sure strokes obliterate Victorian patterns and refashion a façade in modernistic taste. Vacant or partially used upper stories—out of favor for dwelling, office, school, or meeting rooms—are signs of Main Street's impending decline.

Richmond, Virginia, 1969
Edward F. Heite
Historic American Buildings Survey

Reflecting the anti-urban attitudes of the post–World War II era, this modernization of a mid-nineteenth-century commercial building evokes the colonial style of a distant rural past.

Austin, Texas, 1961
First Presbyterian Church
United Press International Photo

As urban renewal projects scatter downtown dwellers, the neighborhood church follows its parishioners to the suburbs. Traditionally, the church tower was the visible symbol of town or city to the surrounding countryside. Now it is the office tower.

Ironically, American optimism, faith in progress, energy, technical innovation—the qualities that built a great urban nation where two centuries before there stood only wilderness—these very same qualities were now galvanized in a vast unbuilding, which, before it was done, would scar and destroy the historic core of many hundreds of towns and cities across the nation.

For nearly two centuries, the federal government had fastidiously avoided involvement in municipal affairs, but it seemed, in the 1940s and 1950s, that only Washington had

230

sufficient power and resources to aid the plight of towns and cities. The Housing Act of 1949 offered federal funds for the clearance of slums and blighted areas—a drastic surgery that slashed out the heart of the troubled urban center as if it were cancerous. And not only were the scars appallingly ugly, but planners realized that new construction alone would not satisfy housing needs or save the city. In place of "urban redevelopment," the law amended in 1954 programmed "urban renewal," recognizing the practical value of rehabilitating older structures in reversing urban decay. But wholesale clearance and rebuilding was an all-too-easy alternative, and this grim practice continued as late as the 1970s.

Federal urban renewal allocations were disbursed to commercial areas, as well as residential areas, in an attempt at a comprehensive solution to the problem of revivifying the life of the city. Through federal-local partnership, irreversible slums were to be demolished, sound structures rehabilitated, business invigorated, municipal services improved, transportation brought up to date and long-range community plans developed. In twenty years, more than two thousand urban renewal projects were undertaken. But in a nation which

Helena, Montana, 1973
John D. Ellingsen

Helena's $6.5 million urban renewal project was planned for "automobility." Building demolition provided new parking spaces, and widened arterial roads offered easier downtown access. "But there are few cars," notes the photographer. "All the stores were torn down."

Somersworth, New Hampshire, 1966
Wide World Photos

In a town as small as Somersworth—population about 9000—the effects of urban renewal are immediate and profound. Demolition of this distinctive 1887 landmark in anticipation of a $1.2 million urban renewal project drastically alters the town's visual image.

Saratoga Springs, New York, 1953
United Press International Photo

As a demonstration of contemporary concepts of "progress," the elegant Grand Union Hotel—lacking certain modern conveniences—is sacrificed for a supermarket.

Flora, Illinois, 1960
Wayne Miller; Magnum

New shopfronts are slapped over old. By 1960, declining standards in construction, materials and maintenance are glaringly obvious.

Denver, Colorado, 1970
William Edmund Barrett; Historic American Buildings Survey

Dating from the early days of Denver's history, this modest commercial
building is a victim of the vast Skyline Urban Renewal.

Bridgeport, Connecticut, 1965
Wide World Photos

Fine dwellings, such as this one, are often the first to fall in urban renewal clearance projects. Bridgeport's downtown revitalization centered around a 52-acre redevelopment area.

Geneva, New York, 1966
Robert Doran

Demolition obliterates older neighborhoods and leaves Main Street stranded. Geneva's comprehensive development plan underlines prevailing American attitudes toward the impoverished center city: "When it appears that a deteriorating or dilapidated structure will not be improved by the owner, when such a structure is in violation of the City's codes and ordinances and when a parking lot in this site would properly serve the nearby area—then the structure should be condemned, razed and parking provided."

234

St. Joseph, Missouri, 1976
William Bennett

The beautiful hotel that once faced St. Joseph's courthouse and a handsome
warehouse behind it were destroyed for urban redevelopment during the
nation's Bicentennial Summer. A high-rise building and a parking facility are
planned for the site.

Hudson, New York, circa 1875
Warren Street, view west from First Street
Rowles Studio Collection

For Hudson, the 1966 National Historic
Preservation Law was tardy. The wheels of
urban renewal, set in motion in 1965, took
several years to slow. And by that time this
block was gone.

Hudson, New York, 1975
Warren Street, view west from First Street
Rowles Studio

236

Buffalo, New York, 1967
United Press International Photo

Urban renewal, and private development at the same scale, shatters the cohesiveness of the late-nineteenth-century city, creating profound shock waves that can continue for years. Many of the nineteenth-century structures seen in this photograph are no longer standing today.

denied its urban history, a nation, in fact, which scorned the city altogether, what could be the result?

At the heart of the urban renewal program was the government's power to acquire vast center-city parcels by exercise of eminent domain. Typically, land was delivered to a local redevelopment agency only after complete clearance, indiscriminately razing tenements and fine old row houses, rotting wood-frame shanties and solid brick schoolhouses. Urban renewal offered the possibility of "correcting past errors," claimed the planners, "for a long overdue rebuilding of cities enslaved to the 20- to 25-foot lot . . . for enlarging the street system surrounding new projects . . . the creation of footways separating pedestrian traffic from the automobile . . . running new highways into the central city's shopping centers . . ."

Intervention brought by the scale of urban renewal, or the developer who followed in its lead, imposed a new geography on the face of the town, sweeping away the incremental growth of history. Sharp edges separated old from new; a single decision erased in a moment those thousands of small decisions that had gradually given the city its form and its

LaCrosse, Wisconsin, 1973
David Plowden

A harsh edge between old and new.

238

substance. The grid was obliterated by new access routes— and the city had yet to learn that bigger and better roads brought more and more cars, and demanded more downtown parking lots.

Time-honored landmarks, at the heart of the town, were sacrificed as obsolete—the courthouse, city hall, hotel and railroad station. Cleared away, too, were those elements that had added texture to the town fabric: the dwellings of the poor, small shops, surviving factories.

The very continuity of the street was broken up—as fewer, but far larger, buildings demanded more space to serve them. Homogeneity replaced diversity. Order obliterated vitality. Space succeeded place.

13. Preservation

Main Street was dying. But the palliative of the fifties—"modernization"—proved woefully inadequate. Remade in the image of the very shopping center that sapped its strength, with serpentine malls, piped-in music, shiny-plastic and pseudo-stone façades, sickly potted trees and gaping parking lots, Main Street was no more vigorous than before. Stop-gap measures only slowed the decline. The energy and enthusiasm needed to restore Main Street as the core of the living town could come only from a commitment to urban living, a feeling of community, a pride in place, a sense of history.

By the early 1960s, the harsh effects of a disappearing heritage were inescapable. "We do not use bombs and powder kegs to destroy irreplaceable structures relating to the story of American civilization. We use the corrosion of neglect or the thrust of bulldozers," grimly announced the Special Commission on Historic Preservation sponsored by the National Conference of Mayors. "A nation can be the victim of amnesia," we were warned. "It can lose the memories of what it was, and thereby lose the sense of what it wants to be."

Taken together, the accelerating rate of growth and changing pattern of urbanization, the enormous power in the hands of politicians, planners and developers, and the traditional American commitment to "progress" that equates protest with sentimentality made the future of the past seem grim indeed. "The threat to our environment is mounting," concluded the Mayors' report. "It will take more than the sounding of periodic alarms to stem the tide."

Nantucket, Massachusetts, 1974
Richard Rifkind

When tourist activity awakened Nantucket from the century-long sleep that
followed the decline of the island's lucrative whaling industry, the challenge
to historic-district designation (in 1955, Nantucket was an early example)
was to preserve the town's extraordinary architectural legacy and yet to
accommodate the needs of the tourist industry. *The Nantucket Historic District Guidebook,* published in 1967, was a brave pioneering effort to establish
detailed guidelines to ensure that future architectural development would be
compatible with historic buildings, regulating building materials, roof pitch
and color, chimney size, door and window types, lights, signs, fences and
flagpoles. To this day, Nantucket is a very special island.
Nevertheless, historic districts across the nation, like Nantucket, recognize
the problems involved in thus limiting individual freedom, and the search
goes on for ways to inculcate a respect for the past that would make such
explicit mandates unnecessary.

Hudson, New York, 1976
Michael Smirnoff
Raymond, Parish, Pine & Weiner, Inc.

The inclusion of Warren Street—since the mid-1960s a designated Urban Renewal site—on the National Register of Historic Places in 1970 forced the bulldozer to a halt. Another result was an innovative solution to the problem of providing low-cost housing while preserving the historic character of the street. The acquisition by the city of façade easements within the Historic District restrains individual owners from making inappropriate alterations and permits the renewal agency to restore and preserve building exteriors. The plan was developed and implemented by Historic Design Associates, Raymond, Parish and Pine, Inc., and the Hudson Urban Renewal Agency.

Salt Lake City, Utah, 1975
Patrick King

Obliterating a block on Main Street, the vast Zion's Co-operative Mercantile Institution shopping center–department store complex is scaled to the massive redevelopment now taking place in downtown Salt Lake City. But as a gesture to Main Street, and to its own history, ZCMI has had reinserted into the new megastructure the cast-iron façade of its 1868 department store, with architect Steven Baird in charge of the painstaking task of restoration and reconstruction.

The eleventh-hour National Historic Preservation Act of 1966 took up this challenge. At the urging of dedicated preservationists, the federal government assumed a major role in the protection of the nation's historic environment. "Congress finds and declares . . . that the historical and cultural foundations of the nation should be preserved as a living part of our community life and development in order to give a sense of orientation to the American people."

The National Register of Historic Places was expanded to include buildings and districts of local as well as national significance. An Advisory Council on Historic Preservation (including the heads of key federal agencies) was empowered to comment on—and thus slow, if not halt—the adverse effects on historic properties by federally funded projects (including urban renewal and highway construction). The states were drawn into partnership with the

243

Newburyport, Massachusetts, 1972 and 1976
William Lane

In Newburyport, the commitment to save the
early-nineteenth-century main street involved a resourceful use of its back side.
To fully utilize the fine three-story brick
buildings fronting on State Street, a sophisticated plan developed by planners Anderson, Notter Associates, at the request of
the municipality, provided for a landscaped
pedestrian plaza at their rear with a free-
standing concrete walkway for easier access
to basements and upper stories.
A comprehensive traffic and parking scheme,
the development of pedestrian places, and
design standards for architectural restoration, graphics, and utilities are important
parts of a larger plan to revive downtown
activity and to enhance the aesthetic and
functional qualities of this historic seaport
town.
The transformation of Newburyport's typical
1960s urban renewal plan—which had
scheduled for demolition the then rapidly
deteriorating State Street—into a historic
redevelopment plan which renews economic
and social life yet preserves the historic
environment is one of the success stories of
the preservation movement.

244

St. Johnsbury House
St. Johnsbury, Vermont
Courtney Fisher; Vermont Division of
Historic Preservation

The announcement by a local bank in August
of 1975 that the foreclosed hotel, the 1850s
St. Johnsbury House, was to be demolished
set off a barrage of opposition which ultimately saved St. Johnsbury House for adap-
tive reuse as a senior citizen's home and
activity center. Not that the action was
accomplished easily. Community ire, organization, professional assistance, a fund-
raising telethon, and federal moneys through
the Vermont Division for Historic Preservation, the Economic Development Administration, and the United States Department of
Housing and Urban Development were all
vitally important components in the ultimate
victory of preserving St. Johnsbury House as
a living Main Street landmark.

federal government through matching grants for historic
preservation. Similar assistance was provided to the National
Trust for Historic Preservation, a private organization,
chartered by Congress, with a missionary role in research, in
education and in stimulating public awareness and concern.
The National Historic Preservation Act set in motion a flood
of legislation and action at federal, state and municipal levels
including historic district ordinances, review of environmental impact, coordination of urban renewal and preservation efforts and local control of long-range planning for community development. Subsequent legislation, executive action and citizen participation have given even greater support
to historic preservation principles within the broader context
of the movement for environmental quality. By July 4, 1976,
as the nation celebrated its bicentennial, more than one thousand historic districts were listed on the National Register of
Historic Places, including Main Streets from Nantucket,
Massachusetts to Mendocino, California.

Georgetown, Colorado, 1976
Ronald Neely; Georgetown Society

Leavenworth Mountain has reigned as a dramatic backdrop for this main street since it was built. Here is a splendid focus for the fine commercial structures accumulated through Georgetown's 1880s silver mining prosperity. Georgetown is listed on the National Register of Historic Places, is designated a National Historic Landmark, and since 1970 has been protected by a historic preservation ordinance, Colorado's first.

Selma, Alabama, 1975
James Rutledge

Nomination of the Water Avenue Historic District to the National Register of Historic Places in 1972 highlighted the need to forestall further deterioration of Selma's riverfront area. Some of the structures lining the fourteen blockfronts along Water Avenue were survivors of the Civil War, others dated from the postwar rebuilding, but many were shabby, deteriorating or vacant. Community effort has made an annual Riverfront Market and Trade Day a big attraction; last year there were 30,000 visitors. Gradually, economic activity is returning, with a mix of specialty shops and night spots that promise a special ambience.

246

Marshall, Michigan, 1972 (upper)
Marshall, Michigan, 1973 (lower)
George Vallillee; Marshall Historical Society

With almost two dozen downtown shops vacant, Marshall was further threatened by the completion in the 1960s of an interstate highway interchange a few miles from the town center. An architectural treasury hardly disturbed since its boom subsided a century earlier, Marshall faced the problem on several fronts: the Chamber of Commerce's sponsorship of a Downtown Restoration Program; the Historical Society's public-awareness program; and to supplement a municipal master plan, the publication of *Marshall: A Plan for Preservation,* supported by a consultant grant from the National Trust for Historic Preservation, funds from the National Park Service through the state of Michigan, and the proceeds of the annual house tour.

This unique building complex—a prim Italianate villa built in 1873 as an addition to an 1866 false-fronted frame drugstore—was menaced by the demand for more parking on the main street. Eight months later, adapted to mixed commercial and residential use, the structure was a major attraction on the Marshall Historical Society 1972 house tour.

Baltimore, Maryland, 1976
Baltimore Department of Housing and
Community Development

Where historic-preservation principles—
with the active support of the press—have
enjoyed a respectable reputation for some
years, renewal schemes quite naturally respect the architectural integrity of older
commercial neighborhoods.

A plan for Gay Street's revitalization was
accomplished by an effective city-federal
partnership, with funds from the Small Business Administration in cooperation with a
local development group. Re-routing traffic,
provision of off-street parking space, the
conversion of a segment of Gay Street to a
pedestrian mall, the renovation of building
façades and the provision of amenities such
as shade trees, benches and water fountains
were important first steps in restoring commercial viability to Baltimore's original
downtown.

The "halo" effect is impressive. The success
of these efforts has inspired the restoration
of a handsome row of townhouses, an historic city market and a venerable fire station.

Moreover, there is a growing understanding that community conservation promotes social stability, that reusing old
buildings supports a sound ecology, that protecting the
special architecture, streetscape and scale of Main Street can
yield solid economic benefits. A revived Main Street preserves history—and also offers aesthetic satisfaction, sociability, comfort, convenience and economy. The very institutions
which once pushed for "progress" at any cost—the Downtown
Development Agency, the Mayor's Office, the planning commission, the chamber of commerce—can now see a future for
the past. Architects and planners, politicians, business and

civic leaders, bankers, developers, historians, students and other citizens find there is much to learn about preservation. The names of some recent conferences reveal current directions in preservation: the Economic Benefits of Preserving Old Buildings (in Seattle) and the Community Preservation Conference (an annual National Trust workshop); the Conference on Small Town Revitalization (in Ithaca, New York) and Planning for Community Conservation (in San Francisco); Back to the City (in St. Paul, Minnesota); Neighborhood Conservation (in New York City); and a conference on the Rehabilitation and Reuse of Your Community's Existing Buildings (in Madison, Wisconsin). From the midwest office of the National Trust for Historic Preservation comes a Main Street "action strategy" that includes consultant services to towns and cities, a national conference, demonstration projects and a practical handbook for Main Street revitalization. The National Park Service, the U.S. Department of Housing and Urban Development, and the Small Business Administration of the U.S. Department of Commerce are among the federal agencies which can provide substantial funding for historic preservation. The National Endowment for the Arts and private foundations have also given impressive support.

Though threats to historic urban environments continue to come from all sides, citizen preservation advocates are gaining expertise and confidence; groups such as *Don't Tear It Down, Inc.* (Washington, D.C.), *New York Landmarks Conservancy, Portland Friends of Cast-Iron Architecture, Community Initiatives, Inc.* (York, Maine), *Preservation of Historic Winchester, Inc.* and hundreds of others across the nation are learning how to use muscle in local decision making. Preservation has become an impressive grass-roots movement, a concern of architects and planners (who have learned that preservation can be profitable), and a recognized profession in itself (more than fifty colleges give courses in historic preservation and at least a dozen offer degree programs in the field). Local history, long the preserve of a small number of antiquarians, has gathered a wide following. Saving a courthouse, restoring a stagecoach inn,

Corning, New York, 1976
Market Street
Norman Mintz; Market Street Restoration
Agency

Hurricane Agnes in 1972 was a disaster for
Corning—but it began the revitalization of
Market Street, a fine ensemble of brick and
terra-cotta commercial buildings, listed on
the National Register of Historic Places.
Revised urban renewal plans called for new
construction which respected the pleasant
late-nineteenth-century scale and streetscape. Federal funds also paid for main
street amenities such as brick-paved sidewalks and honey locust trees at the curbside.
The sense of civic responsibility of the
Corning Glass Works, a major economic
force in the community, resulted in the
funding, through its foundation arm, of the
Market Street Restoration Agency, which
not only provides free design consultation
for façade restoration and improvement, but
develops programs to help the entire community enjoy a renewed and vital main street.
The Corning Historical Society, as well as
business and civic leaders, were convinced
that this town was worth saving—and that
its main street could reflect the quality of
life in the town as a whole.

preserving a commercial row—all enhance the immediacy of
the past for the entire community. Avoiding the all-too-easy
solution of "instant Main Street" in phony colonial or mission
style, small-town Main Streets and main streets in the heart of
great cities find renewed strength in their own unique history.

The old town hall is recycled for new use. Two-story bill-
boards are peeled off shopfronts. Graphics are made to har-
monize with the buildings they adorn. Repair and renovation
are governed by guidelines that stress sympathetic place-
ment, scale, shape, color and texture. The Main Street mall
creates a pedestrian island of commerce, sociability and community. New construction is keyed to historical continuity
without invoking a make-believe town, a museum that stays
in the past, or a fake restoration that puts the lie to history.

A revival of nineteenth-century urbanistic values—a sense
of propriety, a view of the town as an entity, respect for the
rights of the user as pedestrian, patron and citizen—may yet
assure the vitality of twentieth-century Main Street.

Seattle, Washington, 1975
Carleton Knight III

Seen against a mid-twentieth-century background is Seattle's historic business district, built during the 1890s in the small-scale but grand style appropriate to the city's prosperity as a supply center for the Yukon. By the 1960s, down at the heels, the Pioneer Square area seemed doomed for parking lots and a freeway. However, municipal leadership thwarted those plans by enacting tough preservation laws, by establishing a public corporation to finance landmarks restoration, and by success in securing funds for improved lighting, paving and shuttle bus service. The area no longer drains the city's resources; instead it generates jobs, taxes and tourist dollars. ''Pioneer Square has become a symbol and a focal point for Seattle's sense of community pride and togetherness,'' says Mayor Wes Uhlman. And every new preservation effort ensures that Seattle is not just any city, but that ''Seattle has remained, and will remain, Seattle.''

251

Appendix:
Photographing Main Street

Rapid urbanization and development of the art of photography were signal events in nineteenth-century America. Towns and cities caught the photographer's eye from the start; and the photographer's sensibilities played an important part in shaping American city-consciousness. Historic photographs allow one to glimpse Main Street as though through the eyes of contemporaries —to see what they saw, and to feel what they felt. Images of Main Street through time reveal not only change, growth, decay and revival, but evolving attitudes toward Main Street itself.

On September 20, 1839, the *British Queen* steamed into New York harbor, bringing details of the process for fixing an image on a metal plate developed by the Frenchman Louis Daguerre. Within a week, the first American daguerreotype—a street view of Broadway—earned enthusiastic praise, and Americans went on to excel in the daguerrean art. Here was a wonderful mirror of the American reality. For an individualist, the daguerrean portrait proclaimed self-identity; for the romantic, the daguerrean landscape glorified nature; for the nationalist, the daguerrean townscape fostered pride in country.

At first, daguerreotypists were found only in large cities—New York, Philadelphia, Boston. By the mid 1840s, itinerant practitioners, working from horse-drawn "Daguerrean Saloons," fanned out through the New England countryside, taking, and selling, views like the moving of the town hall of Lebanon, New Hampshire, the 1842 Boston fire and the village of Stockbridge in the Berkshire hills.

From makeshift studios on flat-bottomed boats on the Ohio and Mississippi rivers, daguerreotypists viewed the rapidly growing midwestern port cities—Galena, Cincinnati, St. Louis—raw cities, with a messy vitality. Their images featured freshly sawed timber prominent in the foreground, streets bald of trees, the clutter of bales and barrels.

Daguerreotypists rushed west with the forty-niners and witnessed the amazing transformation of helter-skelter miners' shacks into regularly built towns and cities. "On looking at these pictures," wrote a New York City critic reviewing an exhibition of a cyclorama of three hundred of R. H. Vance's daguerreotype views of San Francisco and vicinity in 1851, "one can imagine himself among the hills and mines of California, grasping at the glittering gold that lays before him; wandering over the plains, among the beautiful rivers that flow into the California gulf, or through the streets of San Francisco, Sacramento, or Monterey." The daguerreotype image could not be dismissed as hyperbole; here was indisputable evidence of the changes that were overtaking the American landscape, the nation's prosperity and the extraordinary rapidity of urban growth.

Following the Civil War, a new photographic process was used to record the construction of the transcontinental railway and the towns that mushroomed along the line. Within a few years after its development in the early 1850s, collodion, or wet-plate, photography had made the daguerreotype obsolete. While the daguerreotype was a single image on a copper plate, any number of copies could be printed on paper from a negative image fixed onto a collodion emulsion on the surface of a glass plate. This new method produced photographs in large quantity, large enough to satisfy eager popular curiosity and to foment a national enthusiasm for the westward migration.

Alexander Gardner, official photographer to the Army of the Potomac during the Civil War, photographed along the line of the Eastern Division of the Union Pacific Railway in 1867. Hundreds of views recorded his impressions of the growth of towns on the Kansas prairie. Gardner's method was meticulous, sober and straightforward. He photographed the open plain with its flora and fauna; the distant town; the Main Street; the most prominent structures. No need for dramatic angles—objective fact was amazing enough.

Gardner and other photographers of the wilderness and the frontier West, such as William Henry Jackson and A. J. Russell, took eight-by-ten-inch-, eleven-by-fourteen-inch-, and even larger plates, in scale with the vastness of the West, as well as duplicate sets in small stereograph size. It was the latter that were most widely circulated. Stereographs are small cards, usually about four inches by seven, on which a pair of photographic images are glued side by side. When viewed through a simple optical device, the two images come together as one and give a convincing illusion of depth and immediacy. Collecting stereographs was enormously popular; parlor-chair viewers marveled at the picturesque Adirondacks, the rugged western wilderness, the laying of rails, great new industries, the exploitation of mine, river and forest, the development of the mechanical arts, and Main Streets from New York to California. No less a figure than Oliver Wendell Holmes—whose collection numbered at least ten thousand stereo cards—advocated the systematic collection of stereos as period documents "where all men can find the special forms they particularly desire to see as artists, or as scholars, or as mechanics, or in any other capacity."

By the 1870s, even the smallest community could claim the services of a photographer specializing in stereograph views of town and countryside. Some twenty or thirty views made up an incredibly detailed village portrait. First, the vista of the town from a nearby hill. Then the village center, with its post office and general store, and several views of Main Street—looking east, looking west, near the old cemetery, the ancient elms. Churches, public buildings, landmarks, dwellings of the town fathers, mills and tanneries, side roads, and even the extreme end of Main Street—all achieved immortality through his camera.

The largest publisher of American stereo views was the firm of E. Anthony, whose New York emporium issued more than ten thousand titles in the years between 1859 and 1881. Victorians bought stereos for the information they gave, almost as we buy newspapers today. Stereos were also purchased as souvenirs, given as gifts, offered as premiums and sold by canvassers. The wholesale price in 1881 probably averaged less than twenty cents a card. After the early 1880s, stereo prints were made from gelatin dry plates—more sensitive to light and needing no tedious preparation—and they continued to enjoy popularity into the first decade of the twentieth century.

Town and city views were also valued in photograph albums and in printed books bound together with photographs. About the earliest of these was the *San Francisco Album,* published in 1856 by Herre and Bauer, with photographs by George F. Fardon. The book or album devoted to a complete town portrait, such as *Marlboro, Illustrated* (1881), showed not only the face of the town—its Main Street and important buildings—but also its in-

dustries, edges, alleys and back streets. These volumes proliferated in response to heightened interest in local history after the
centennial celebration.

Important technological improvements of this period included
more sensitive film, flexible roll film, the automatic shutter and
the hand-held camera. With the shorter exposure time that these
improvements permitted, Main Street action shots were now
easily taken, and an army of amateurs joined the professionals.

The development of photomechanical printing methods such
as photogravure—in which the image is printed from a photo-
graphically engraved copper plate—or the Albertype process
(known also as collotype, heliotype or artotype)—in which the
image, fixed in gelatin held on the surface of a glass or metal
plate, is used to print in colored ink on paper—permitted editions
as large as two thousand. After 1890, books illustrated with half-
tones—a process in which the photographic image, broken into
fine dots through a screen, is etched onto a metal plate and
printed along with type—were commonly commissioned by
chambers of commerce or local trade associations as booster items.
These were cheap, and issued in large numbers, but both the
quantity and the quality of photographic images showed a
marked decline.

Surely, no more telling measure of Main Street's symbolic
significance in the period preceding World War I is its prominence in photographic imagery. Favorite views, captured by
itinerant photographers employed by souvenir-view companies,
were choice Main Street corners, Main Street from the courthouse
square, and City Beautiful improvements such as fountains, parks
and public buildings. Among the largest of the firms specializing
in souvenir views was the Detroit Publishing Company. William
Henry Jackson, pioneer photographer of the western frontier, had
joined the firm in 1897 as part-owner and chief photographer.
Jackson himself photographed townscape and landscape on the
Atlantic coast from Virginia to Florida, the Colorado Rockies, the
Texas Panhandle and the Southwest, and trained a fleet of photographers whose combined output probably exceeded 100,000
images, providing an extraordinarily detailed visual archive of the
American environment over the period of a generation. Pride in
place is obvious; hardly surprising is the typical postcard in-
scription: "Wish you were here!"

Tender portraits of Main Street in its golden age—1890–1920—
portraits depicting the humble as well as the grand, were the work
of local commercial photographers from Orange, New Jersey;

Stillwater, Minnesota; Pendleton, Oregon, and hundreds of towns and cities across the country. Photographers like Frank P. Jewett, John Runk and Walter Scott Bowman used spare-time moments over the course of a career to create an *oeuvre* of thousands of images and brilliantly illuminate the texture of Main Street through time. How Main Street looked, what went on, the changes that took place, were matters of keen interest to these sensitive observers.

A few firms continued to take souvenir views, and postcard collecting was still popular but the preoccupation with Main Street was dissipated by the World War I era. The photographic aesthetic of the '20s and '30s was dominated by a concern for personal vision—Alfred Stieglitz's portraits of clouds, Charles Sheeler's abstractions of Pennsylvania barns and industrial architecture, Paul Strand's studies of sunlight on adobe. America looked inward, America looked to Europe—but not at Main Street. Only as part of the New Deal public works projects did Main Street again achieve prominence in the public view.

In 1935, in an effort to create favorable propaganda for the controversial work of the Resettlement Administration (later the Farm Security Administration), Rexford Tugwell hired Roy Stryker, a one-time Columbia University associate of his and a pioneer in the didactic use of photographs, as Chief of the Historical Section. Stryker branched out far from his initial mandate to document the problems of rural poverty. Over the next seven years, a team of brilliant photographers—including, at one time or another, such gifted artists as Walker Evans, Dorothea Lange, John Vachon, Marion Post Wolcott and Russell Lee—amassed more than a quarter-million photographs covering every aspect of American life, but with close scrutiny of the small-town experience. In the spring of 1936, as a result of a meeting with Robert Lynd, coauthor of *Middletown*, the classic sociological study of the American town, Stryker circulated among his photographers elaborate "shooting scripts" for scenes to be photographed for "American Background": "Photographs showing the various ways that different groups spend their evenings. . . . Where can people meet? Well-to-do. Poor. Street corners . . . Looking Down My Street . . . How do people look? . . . in towns of various sizes . . . 1500, 25,000 to 30,000, 100,000 . . . Small towns under war conditions . . ." Main Street is merely the stage set for these small-town dramas, although a few of the Farm Security Administration photographers—especially the brilliant

256

Walker Evans (himself an avid postcard collector)—give vernacular architecture and humble streetscape a leading role.

But the intense emotions of the 1940s generated the taste for action views. Photojournalists from *Life, Look* and the wire services saw traffic jams, fire, crime, riots, demolition and destruction. Gone was the feeling for lived-in buildings, an appreciation for simple function, a sense of streetscape, an understanding of the meaning of Main Street in the life of the nation. As neglect and decay eroded the urban environment, photographers averted their eyes from its suffering.

Finally, in the late 1960s, the National Historic Preservation Act spurred the National Register program and the Historic American Buildings Survey. The photographer returned to Main Street—there, once again, to find beauty and ugliness, the grandeur of the ordinary and the legacy of history.

Selected Bibliography

The study of a Main Street should begin with an inventory of Main Street structures, local records, reminiscences, memorabilia and photographic collections, and extend to a variety of disciplines including urban history, architectural history, social history, and the history of town planning, technology and transportation. In addition to the standard works on American history, particularly useful is the *American Guide Series*, an undertaking begun by the Works Project Administration in the 1930s, which includes separate volumes for each of the states as well as a number of others devoted to particular cities and areas. Some periodicals of interest are: *Atlantic Monthly* (1857–), *The American City* (1909–), *Century* (1870–1930), *The Craftsman* (1901–1916), *Landscape* (1951–1975), *Harper's* (1850–), *Historic Preservation* (1949–), *Journal of the Society of Architectural Historians* (1941–) and the *Scientific American Supplement* (1876–1919).

The books and articles listed below provide further background material.

Anderson, Sherwood, *Poor White*, New York, 1920.

———, *Hello Towns!* New York, 1929.

———, *Home Town*, New York, 1940.

———, *Memoirs*, New York, 1942.

Andrews, Ralph W., *Picture Gallery Pioneers*, Seattle, 1964.

Angle, Paul McC., *Prairie State: Impressions of Illinois, 1673–1967*, Chicago, 1968.

Atherton, Lewis, *Main Street on the Middle Border*, Bloomington, 1954.

———, "The Middle Way: the Small American City," *Landscape*, Autumn 1957.

Austin, Mary, *A Woman of Genius,* New York, 1912.

Barber, J. W., and Howe, H., *Our Whole Country or the Past and Present of the United States, Historical and Descriptive,* Cincinnati, 1861.

Bell, William A., *New Tracks in North America,* London, 1869.

Birbeck, Morris, *Notes on a Journey to America from the Coast of Virginia to the Territory of Illinois,* London, 1856.

Blake, Peter, *God's Own Junkyard,* New York, 1964.

Boorstin, Daniel J., *The Americans: The Colonial Experience,* New York, 1958.

———, *The Americans: The National Experience,* New York, 1965.

———, *The Americans: The Democratic Experience,* New York, 1973.

Brook, H. Ellington, *An Illustrated History of Los Angeles County,* Chicago, 1889.

Bryce, James, *The American Commonwealth,* New York, 1891.

Burchard, John, and Bush-Brown, Albert, *The Architecture of America: A Social and Cultural History,* Boston, 1961.

Cable, George W., *John March: Southerner,* New York, 1903.

Callow, Alexander B., Jr., ed., *American Urban History,* New York, 1969.

Chase, Edwin Percy, "Forty Years on Main Street," *Iowa Journal of History and Politics,* July 1936.

Coke, Van Deren, ed., *One Hundred Years of Photographic History,* Albuquerque, 1975.

Condit, Carl, *American Building: Materials and Techniques from the First Colonial Settlement,* Chicago, 1967.

Cravath, J. R., "The Replacement of Old Style Street Lamps and Lighting Fixtures," *The American City,* January 1916.

Cullen, Gordon, *The Concise Townscape,* New York, 1971.

Curti, Merle, *The Roots of American Loyalty,* New York, 1946.

Darrah, William C., *A History of Stereographs in America and Their Collection,* Gettysburg, 1964.

Davidson, Marshall, *Life in America,* New York, 1951.

Davol, Ralph, *A Handbook on American Pageantry,* Taunton, 1914.

Depew, Chauncey M., *One Hundred Years of American Commerce,* New York, 1895.

DeRousiers, Paul, *American Life,* New York, 1893.

De Tocqueville, Alexis, *Journey to America,* New Haven, 1959.

Dick, Everett, *The Lure of the Land,* Lincoln, 1970.

Dunbar, Seymour, *History of Travel in America,* Indianapolis, 1915.

Dunlap, George A., *The City in the American Novel, 1789–1900,* Philadelphia, 1934.

Dwight, Theodore, *Things as They Are,* New York, 1834.

Dwight, Timothy, *Travels in New England and New York,* New Haven, 1821.

Evans, Walker, "Main Street Looking North from Courthouse Square," *Fortune,* May 1948.

——, "When 'Downtown' Was a Beautiful Mess," *Fortune,* January 1962.

Ferber, Edna, *Cimarron,* New York, 1930.

Finley, David, *History of the National Trust,* Washington, 1963.

Fisher, Dorothy Canfield, *Hillsboro People,* New York, 1915.

Fitch, James Marston, *Architecture and the Aesthetics of Plenty,* New York, 1961.

——, *American Building: The Historical Forces That Shaped It,* vol. 1, New York, 1966.

——, *American Building: The Environmental Forces That Shaped It,* vol. 2, New York, 1972.

——, "Environmental Aspects of the Preservation of Historic Urban Areas," prepared for Research and Development Branch, Center for Housing, Building and Planning, United Nations, New York, 1971.

Flagg, Edmund, *The Far West,* New York, 1838.

Fletcher, Henry J., "The Doom of the Small Town," *The Forum,* March 1895.

Flink, James J., *The Car Culture,* Cambridge, 1975.

Florin, Lambert, *A Guide to Western Ghost Towns,* Seattle, 1967.

Francis, George E., "Photography as an Aid to Local History," *Proceedings of the American Antiquarian Society,* Worcester, April 1888.

Gale, Zona, *Civic Improvement in Little Towns,* Washington, 1913.

Garvan, Anthony, *Architecture and Town Planning in Colonial Connecticut,* New Haven, 1951.

Glaab, Charles N., *The American City: A Documentary History,* Homewood, 1963.

Glaab, Charles N., and Brown, A. Theodore, *A History of Urban America,* London, 1967.

Gowans, Alan, *Images of American Living: Four Centuries of Architecture and Furniture as Cultural Expression,* Philadelphia, 1964.

Green, Constance McL., *The Rise of Urban America,* New York, 1965.

Hawthorne, Nathaniel, *Main Street,* Canton, 1901.

Helper, Hinton, *The Impending Crisis of the South: How to Meet It,* New York, 1857.

Herron, Ima, *The Small Town in American Literature,* Durham, 1939.

Hilton, George W., and Due, John F., *Electric Interurban Railways in America,* Stanford, 1960.

Holbrook, Stewart, *The Yankee Exodus,* Seattle, 1968.

Hosmer, Charles B., *Presence of the Past,* New York, 1965.

Hurley, F. Jack, *Portrait of a Decade. Roy Stryker and the Development of Documentary Photography,* Baton Rouge, 1972.

Jackson, John Brinckerhoff, *American Space: The Centennial Years, 1865–1876,* New York, 1972.

Jacobs, Jane, *The Death and Life of Great American Cities,* New York, 1961.

Jewett, Sarah Orne, *The Country Doctor,* Boston, 1884.

Jensen, Merrill, *Regionalism in America,* Madison, 1951.

Jones, Charles Colcock, *The Dead Towns of Georgia,* Savannah, 1878.

Kirkland, Edward C., *Men, Cities, and Transportation: A Study in New England History, 1820–1900,* Cambridge, 1948.

Lindsay, Vachel, *Village Magazine,* Springfield, Ill., 1920.

Lohof, Bruce A. "The Service Station in America: The Evolution of a Vernacular Form," *Industrial Archeology,* Spring 1974.

Lossing, Benson John, *The American Centenary: A History of the Progress of the Republic of the United States During the First One Hundred Years of Its Existence,* Philadelphia, 1876.

Lynch, Kevin, *The Image of the City,* Cambridge, 1960.

———, *What Time Is This Place?* Cambridge, 1972.

McKelvey, Blake, *The Urbanization of America, 1860–1915,* New Brunswick, 1963.

———, *The Emergence of Metropolitan America, 1915–1966,* New Brunswick, 1968.

———, *The City in American History,* New York, 1969.

Manning, Warren H., "The History of Village Improvement in the United States," *The Craftsman,* February 1904.

Masters, Edgar Lee, *Across Spoon River,* New York, 1969.

Muir, John, *Steep Trails,* New York, 1918.

Mumford, Lewis, *Sticks and Stones,* New York, 1955.

———, *The City in History,* New York, 1961.

Murphy, Raymond E., *The American City: An Urban Geography,* New York, 1966.

Nairn, Ian, *The American Landscape,* New York, 1965.

National Trust, "Legal Techniques in Historic Preservation," Selected Papers from the Conference on Legal Techniques in Preservation Sponsored by the National Trust for Historic Preservation, Washington, 1971.

Nevins, Allan, *American Social History as Recorded by British Travellers*, New York, 1923.

Newhall, Beaumont, *The Daguerreotype in America*, New York, 1961.

Newhall, Beaumont, and Edkins, Diana, *William Henry Jackson*, Fort Worth, 1974.

Nolen, John, *Comprehensive Planning for Small Towns and Villages*, Boston, 1911.

———, *New Towns for Old: Achievement in Civic Improvement in Some American Small Towns and Neighborhoods*, Boston, 1927.

Nolting, Orin F., *The Parking Problem in Central Business Districts*, Chicago, 1938.

Northrop, B. G., *Rural Improvement*, New Haven, 1880.

———, "The Work of Village Improvement Societies," *The Forum*, March 1895.

Novotny, Ann, ed., *Picture Sources 3. Collection of Prints and Photographs in the U.S. and Canada*, New York, 1975.

Olmsted, Frederick Law, "The Limits to City Beautification—A Reply to an Inquiry," *The American City*, May 1910.

Paullin, Charles O., *Atlas of Historical Geography of the United States*, Washington, 1932.

Quiett, Glen Chesney, *They Built the West*, New York, 1934.

Rae, John B., *The Road and the Car in American Life*, Cambridge, 1971.

Rasmussen, Steen Eiler, *Towns and Buildings Described in Drawings and Words*, Cambridge, 1969.

Reps, John W., *The Making of Urban America: A History of City Planning in the United States*, Princeton, 1965.

Richardson, Albert Deane, *Beyond the Mississippi*, Hartford, 1867.

Ridge, Martin, and Billington, Rae Allen, *A Documentary History of Westward Expansion*, New York, 1969.

Robinson, Charles Mulford, *The Improvement of Towns and Cities*, New York, 1901.

———, *Modern Civic Art or the City Made Beautiful*, New York, 1918.

Rudisill, Richard, *Mirror Image*, Albuquerque, 1971.

Russell, Charles, *Diary of a Visit to the United States of America in the Year 1883*, New York, 1910.

Sakolski, Aaron M., *The Great American Land Bubble: The Amazing Story of Land-Grabbing, Speculations, and Booms from Colonial Days to the Present Time*, New York, 1932.

Santmyer, Helen, *Ohio Town*, Columbus, 1962.

Schlesinger, Arthur, *The Rise of the City, 1878–1898*, New York, 1933.

Scott, Jessup W., "The Great West," *De Bow's Review*, July, 1853.

Scott, Mel, *American City Planning Since 1890*, Berkeley, 1969.

Scully, Vincent J., *American Architecture and Urbanism*, New York, 1969.

Shaler, Nathaniel Southgate, *American Highways: A Popular Account of Their Condition and of the Means by Which They May Be Bettered*, New York, 1896.

Silverberg, Robert, *Ghost Towns of the American West*, New York, 1968.

Smith, Page, *As a City upon a Hill: The Town in American History*, New York, 1966.

Smith, Warren Hunting, *An Elegant But Salubrious Village: A Portrait of Geneva, New York*, Geneva, 1931.

Stover, John F., *American Railroads*, Chicago, 1961.

Stowe, Harriet Beecher, *Old Town Folks*, Boston, 1869.

Strauss, Anselm, *Images of the American City*, New York, 1961.

Stryker, Roy E., and Wood, Nancy, *In This Proud Land: America 1935–1943 as Seen in the FSA Photographs*, Boston, 1973.

Sturgis, Russell, "Grass and Trees in Towns," *Scribner's Magazine*, November 1904.

Sullivan, Louis, *The Autobiography of an Idea*, New York, 1926.

Sutter, Ruth E., *The Next Place You Come To: A Historical Introduction to Communities in North America*, Englewood Cliffs, 1973.

Taft, Robert, *Photography and the American Scene: A Social History*, New York, 1938.

Tarkington, Booth. *The Magnificent Ambersons*, New York, 1918.

Trewartha, Glenn, "Types of Rural Settlements in Colonial America," *Geographical Review*, October 1946.

Tryon, Warren S., *A Mirror for Americans: Life and Manners in the United States 1790–1870 as Recorded by American Travelers*, Chicago, 1952.

Tuckerman, Henry T., *America and Her Commentators*, New York, 1864.

Tunnard, Christopher. *The Modern American City*, Princeton, 1968.

Tunnard, Christopher, and Reed, Henry Hope, *American Skyline*,

New York, 1956.

Twain, Mark, *Roughing It,* Hartford, 1872.

———, *Life on the Mississippi,* Boston, 1883.

U.S. Conference of Mayors, Special Committee on Historic Preservation, *With Heritage So Rich,* New York, 1966.

U.S. Department of Commerce, Bureau of the Census, *Historical Statistics of the U.S.,* Washington, 1975.

Venturi, Robert, Brown, Denise Scott, and Izenour, Steven, *Learning from Las Vegas,* Cambridge, 1972.

Wade, Richard C., *The Urban Frontier: The Rise of Western Cities, 1790–1830,* Cambridge, 1959.

Wakstein, Allen M., *The Urbanization of America,* Boston, 1970.

Ward, Julius H., "The Revival of Our Country Towns," *New England Magazine,* November 1889.

Waring, George Edwin, *Village Improvements and Farm Villages,* Boston, 1877.

Warner, Sam Bass, Jr., *The Urban Wilderness: A History of the American City,* New York, 1972.

Webb, Todd, *Gold Strikes and Ghost Towns,* New York, 1961.

Weimer, David, *City and Country in America,* New York, 1962.

Welling, William, *Collectors' Guide to Nineteenth Century Photographs,* New York, 1976.

Wescott, Glenway, *Good-bye Wisconsin,* New York, 1928.

Whiffen, Marcus, *American Architecture Since 1780,* Cambridge, 1969.

White, Harry E., Jr., "A Discussion of Historic Districts Legislation," *Columbia Law Review,* April 1963.

White, William Allen, *The Autobiography of William Allen White,* New York, 1946.

Wilson, James A., *Urban Renewal: The Record and the Controversy,* Cambridge, 1966.

Woestemeyer, Ina Faye, *The Westward Movement: A Book of Readings on Our Changing Frontier,* New York, 1939.

Zueblin, Charles, "A Decade of Civic Improvement," Address at St. Paul, Minnesota, 1902.

———, *American Municipal Progress,* New York, 1916.

Index of Places